HEALER OF A BROKEN HEART

A MINISTER'S GUIDE TO EULOGIES

WHAT READERS ARE SAYING ABOUT
Healer of a Broken Heart

"A book for every minister's library! With the experience and expertise gained over decades of bereavement services, Rev. Nichole L. Edness, in *Healer of a Broken Heart*, boldly enlightens and equips the minister on what makes for a truly successful eulogy. She makes a case that the eulogy is not so much about the words the bereaved will hear. Rather, with the Holy Spirit's guidance, the eulogy, from crafting to delivery, is about delivering the words the broken-hearted bereaved needs to feel. Whether a new minister or one that has been at it a while, there's something to gain here for any and everyone called upon to deliver a message to those in sorrow."

~Bishop Brenda C. Huger Hazel, D.Min.

"*Healer of a Broken Heart* is a masterclass in crafting eulogies that are powerful, poignant, and deeply soul-stirring. Rev. Nichole Edness is divinely gifted to minister to the grieving heart. She has poured her decades of experience as a minister to the bereaved into this informative, insightful, inspirational book. She offers wisdom, comfort, and practical tools for those called to speak life and healing into moments of deepest sorrow. *Healer of a Broken Heart* is essential reading for anyone who seeks to minister with empathy and eloquence to those navigating the pain of loss."

~Rev. Dr. Debbye Turner Bell, CEO & Founder, Debbye Turner Bell Consulting; Staff Pastor; Miss America 1990

"This book is a gift to clergy and anyone who seeks to expand their capacity for compassion towards anyone grieving. When death visits us, we remember the healing hugs from friends more than we do the deep platitudes from well-meaning people. *Healer of a Broken Heart* book is like a healing hug for those seeking to comfort others and for those who still need to be comforted on their journey of grief."

~Rev. Reginald W. Sharpe Jr., Senior Pastor,
Fellowship Missionary Baptist Church

"*Healer of a Broken Heart* is a transformative resource that equips faith leaders to provide spiritual care for families and communities in their darkest hours. With wisdom and compassion, this book offers essential guidance for those called to minister to the brokenhearted. It is required reading for anyone serious about the sacred work of healing and hope."

~Rev. Stephen A. Green, Senior Pastor,
The Greater Allen A.M.E. Cathedral of New York

HEALER OF A BROKEN HEART
A MINISTER'S GUIDE TO EULOGIES

BY:

NICHOLE L. EDNESS

Copyright © 2025 by Nichole L. Edness

All rights reserved. Except permitted under the U.S. Copyright Act of 1976, no part of this publication may be used, reproduced, distributed or transmitted by in any form or by any means, graphic, electronic or mechanical or stored in a database or retrieval system, without the prior written permission to the publisher except in the case of brief quotations embodied in critical articles and reviews.

Unless otherwise indicated, Scriptures are taken from the Holy Bible, New International Version®, NIV® Copyright © 1973, 1978, 1984, 2011 by Biblica, Inc.™ Used by permission. All rights reserved worldwide.

Scripture quotations marked (NRSV) are taken from the New Revised Standard Version Bible, copyright © 1989 National Council of the Churches of Christ in the United States of America. Used by permission. All rights reserved.

Scripture quotations marked (TLB) are taken from The Living Bible, copyright © 1971 by Tyndale House Foundation. Used by permission of Tyndale House Publishers, Inc., Carol Stream, Illinois 60188. All rights reserved.

Scripture taken from the New King James Version®. Copyright © 1982 by Thomas Nelson. Used by permission. All rights reserved.

Scripture taken from the Amplified Bible, Classic Edition, Copyright © 1954, 1958, 1962, 1964, 1965, 1987 by The Lockman Foundation. Used by permission. All rights reserved.

Scripture quotations marked (NLT) are taken from the Holy Bible, New Living Translation, copyright © 1996, 2004, 2015 by Tyndale House Foundation. Used by permission of Tyndale House Publishers, Inc., Carol Stream, Illinois 60188. All rights reserved.

Scripture quotations marked (JUB) are taken from the Jubilee Bible 2000, Copyright © 2013, 2020 by Ransom Press International. Used by permission. All rights reserved.

Vine Publishing's name and logo are trademarks of Vine Publishing, Inc.

ISBN: 979-8-9891446-4-8 (paperback)
ISBN: 979-8-9891446-5-5 (e-book)

Library of Congress Cataloging-in-Publication Data
Library of Congress Control Number: 2025903820

Published by Vine Publishing, Inc.
New York, NY
www.vinepublish.com

Printed in the United States of America

DEDICATION

This book is dedicated to the most amazing woman that I know, my mom, W. Patricia Stewart. Mom, you are the epitome of resilience, courage, and strength. Thank you for your unconditional love and support.

ACKNOWLEDGMENTS

It is imperative that I first acknowledge and thank the God of all creation—the One who gave me the desire to write this book. I give God all the glory and praise.

To my son, Nicholas Alexander Edness: Whatever God places on your heart to accomplish, do not be afraid. God will grant you all the resources you will need. I love you eternally.

To my sister, Deborah Smith: I love you and appreciate you. You are the best sister a person could ever have. Thank you for supporting me all my life. You have been my number one cheerleader. You have always been there, and I want you to know that you mean the world to me. Thank you.

To Pastor Emeritus, the Rev. Dr. Floyd H. Flake: Thank you for the times when you would drop into my office with an encouraging word. Thank you for your gentle nudges when you would say, "Nikki, you should write a book of your eulogies." Little did you know that God used you to confirm this book. I am forever grateful for your kindness and support.

To Pastor Emeritus, the Rev. Dr. Elaine M. Flake: Thank you for your continuous support. Thank you for always giving me the go-ahead to explore ministry and grow as a leader. Thank you for always being willing to listen, guide, and engage in meaningful conversations that have blessed me more than words can say.

To my mentor, the Rev. Dr. Brenda Huger Hazel: You believed in me when I didn't believe in myself, thank you. Thank you for being a friend, a confidante—someone who I can always depend on for sound advice. You have been a pivotal part of my journey from a babe in Christ to ordained ministry. Thank you for the years of laboring in prayer for me and the call that was upon my life. I sincerely do not have enough words to say thank you.

To my good sister-friends who played an integral role in shaping this book, Rev. Dr. Lezlie Austin-Kennedy, Rev. Dr. Debbye Turner Bell, Rev. Judy Davis, Rev. Adrian I. Faulk, Rev. Dr. C. Aldrena Mabry, and my neice, Patrice L. Smith: Thank you for your friendship, love, and prayers. I am grateful for the times we have had laughing, crying, sharing, and supporting each other. My heart is filled with gratitude for you all. From the depths of my heart, thank you.

To my coach and publisher, Taneki Dacres: This book was waiting for you and me to connect. With God's grace and in the many hours we have spent working on this book, you have encouraged and supported me. Your writing expertise is incredible, and I am forever

ACKNOWLEDGMENTS

grateful for the patience and wisdom you have poured out during this process.

Last, but surely not least, thank you to everyone who has loved me, supported me, and prayed for and with me. Thank you and God bless you.

FOREWORD
~ REV. DR. ELAINE M. FLAKE ~

For over twenty-five years, the Reverend Nichole Edness has had the burden and the privilege of ministering to the bereaved in our church and community. Hundreds have been blessed, and their lives have been enriched by her concern and passion for those who are in the throes of working through the pain that comes with the loss of a loved one. She has empathized with them, assisted them with funeral arrangements and obituary preparation, and also followed up with them with grief support sessions. But an integral part of her ministry has been formulating and preaching eulogies.

To be sure, preaching is an art that requires creativity, contextualization, and commitment to Christ and Bible, and preaching eulogies requires all of that and more. The eulogist is charged with the task of celebrating the life of the deceased, comforting the bereaved, and challenging every listener to embrace the possibility of living life to the fullest, even after loss. In this very unique work, Reverend Edness has very thoughtfully gifted the reader with a collection of eulogies that will both inspire and instruct.

    I am confident that this book will assist in the craft of structuring and delivering eulogies that pay tribute to the deceased and move the eulogist and listeners closer to God.

PREFACE

There is an old adage that says, "In this world nothing can be said to be certain, except death and taxes." As long as we are living on this earth, we will indeed have to face the dreaded responsibility of paying taxes. Taxes are inevitable . . . and so is death. Death will come knocking for every creature on the earth. We never know when. We don't know how. But we can rest assured that at some point, our spirits will depart from our mortal bodies and we will cease to exist among the living on the earth.

Death is inevitable, and daily, many are faced with dealing with the reality of departed loved ones. It is during these difficult seasons of life that I believe God is asking, "Whom shall I send? And who will go for us?" (Isaiah 6:8 NIV). What will your response be? Will you respond, "Here am I. Send me to wipe the tears from the eyes of the bereaved?" Will you respond, "Send me to bring comfort . . . Send me to be a healer of a broken heart?" What will your response be when God calls you to be light and life in the midst of darkness and death? How will you magnify God, honor the deceased, and comfort saved and unsaved loved ones? How will you answer the call to minister to the bereaved?

It was July 1999 when I responded, "Here am I. Send me." I was a recent graduate from Colgate Rochester Crozer Divinity School and had returned to my home church, The Greater Allen A.M.E. Cathedral of New York, to enter into full-time ministry as the Minister of Membership Nurture. In this position, it was my responsibility to coordinate ministry to the sick and shut-in members of the church, ensuring that each member received a visit from both a minister and an officer of the church once a month. It was also my responsibility to oversee ministry to the bereaved. This involved helping the bereaved prepare a home going service for their loved one that included a eulogy and a committal service.

While I knew that I was called to ordained ministry, the reality was that my first six months ministering to the bereaved were excruciating and emotionally painful. In these first few months, a twenty-one-year-old was hit by a car and died, a baby was stillborn in the ninth month, and a thirty-five-year-old died from cancer. It was nonstop funeral services. By the sixth month, I was emotionally drained and found myself in a deep dark place. I began to question the call and my response. I thought, *Maybe I did not hear the true direction of God for my life. Maybe this ministry was not for me.* I questioned, *Why isn't God healing the cancer patients? Why did children have to die without*

PREFACE

the opportunity to have an earthly life? Thought after thought, question after question: By the sixth month, I was frazzled and afraid of the ministry. But I had a good friend praying for me, and prayer works.

My fears were quelled and nerves calmed with one faithful word from God. I remember it vividly: God spoke to me through Isaiah 61:1–3 (NIV) and I was never the same.

> *The Spirit of the Sovereign Lord is on me,*
> *because the Lord has anointed me*
> *to proclaim good news to the poor.*
> *He has sent me to bind up the brokenhearted,*
> *to proclaim freedom for the captives*
> *and release from darkness for the prisoners,*
> *to proclaim the year of the Lord's favor*
> *and the day of vengeance of our God,*
> *to comfort all who mourn,*
> *and provide for those who grieve in Zion—*
> *to bestow on them a crown of beauty*
> *instead of ashes,*
> *the oil of joy*
> *instead of mourning,*
> *and a garment of praise*
> *instead of a spirit of despair.*
> *They will be called oaks of righteousness,*
> *a planting of the Lord*
> *for the display of his splendor.*

This *rhema* Word from our faithful God entered my heart and quickened my spirit, and I knew beyond a shadow of a doubt that I was assigned and anointed by the Sovereign Lord to minister to the bereaved. This conviction was settled in my soul. I had the God-given ability to help the brokenhearted journey through their grief.

It is almost hard to believe that it has been twenty-five years that I have been providing ministry to the bereaved. Twenty-five years filled with celebrations of life, tears, joy, comfort, healing, and salvation. Twenty-five years of providing comfort to the saved and the unsaved, members and nonmembers. Twenty-five years of preparing eulogies for all ages—believers and unbelievers. Twenty-five years of preparing services for an average of seventy to eighty people per year. Twenty-five years of experiencing the faithfulness of God, through God's Word, to bring joy and comfort in the midst of life's sorrow. Twenty-five years that have prepared me to give birth to this book, *Healer of a Broken Heart*.

Along with my responsibilities as the Minister of Membership Nurture for my church, I am also honored to be the minister in charge of guiding and training new ministers in sermon preparation and delivery prior to their initial sermon. It was while in this role as a mentor to new ministers that I discovered that one of the most daunting tasks for novice ministers is the preparation of eulogies. Many new ministers had no idea where to start and even questioned their emotional stability to provide comfort for grieving families. As I guided each minister along the way, I eventually realized that they needed further guidance outside of our mentoring relationship, and thus, *Healer of a Broken Heart: A Minister's Guide to Eulogies* was born.

PREFACE

Healer of a Broken Heart is a much-needed resource guide for preparing effective and well-written eulogies. In my twenty-five years of bereavement ministry, I have had to eulogize people from all walks of life, ages, cultures, and beliefs. The insight, guidance, and eulogies I provide in this book are given to assist you when you are faced with the inevitable task of ministering to grieving souls. The book is broken down into seven chapters that address everything from the challenges ministers will face (chapter 1), to pre-eulogy preparation including the dos and don'ts (chapter 2), to examples of eulogies for children, women, men, and the elderly (chapters 3, 4, 5, and 6). As you navigate through the pages, you will notice that each eulogy is broken down into sections with annotations provided. In addition, for some of the eulogies, I provide a synopsis of the deceased and the circumstances surrounding their passing. For the privacy of the families, I have changed some of the names of the deceased, but it was necessary for me to provide some background information as you may be faced with a similar circumstance. In chapter 7, I provide my final takeaways and encouragement to help you do the work that God has called you to do. Also, note that although separated by categories, the eulogies are interchangeable for any gender. Finally, in the appendix of this book, you will find a sample Order of Service and a Funeral Arrangement Intake Form.

It is important to note here that it is not my intention for you to simply copy and use these eulogies for your services, but I hope that through the information and guidance provided, any feelings of uncertainty or intimidation about ministering to the bereaved would disappear and in its place will reside strength, confidence, and courage that comes from the indwelling of the Holy Spirit. It is my hope that you will be enlightened, informed, and equipped to prepare powerful, comforting eulogies for the brokenhearted.

My years in ministry have taught me that bereavement ministry does not consist solely of honoring the life of the elderly and providing comfort to their family, but in fact in bereavement ministry, we will be called to eulogize the young mother who died from cancer, the husband who died suddenly, the child that died tragically, and the babies who were stillborn. Death is inevitable, and as ministers, it takes the hand of God upon our lives to provide comfort to the crushed in spirit.

I don't know where you are in your ministry. Perhaps you are called to the ministry of bereavement and perhaps you are not. Either way, at some point in your ministry, as one called to be God's mouthpiece, you will be called upon to provide ministry to mourning loved ones. It is at that point I hope that you will use *Healer of a Broken Heart: A Minister's Guide to Eulogies* to assist you in your preparation. It is my prayer that as you read this book, the Lord will enrich your soul and grant you the wisdom, knowledge, understanding, compassion, and love necessary to minister effectively to the emotionally weary, brokenhearted souls. God bless.

> "If I can help somebody, then my living is not in vain."

Chapter 1

THE BURDENSOME JOY OF BEREAVEMENT

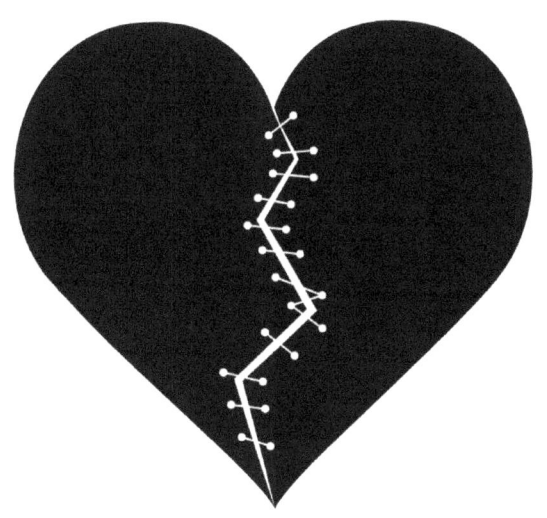

THE BURDENSOME JOY OF BEREAVEMENT

Death will come knocking at our doors as religious leaders. I am not referring to your personal death, but the death of a coworker, the death of one of your faithful members, the death of a member of the community, the death of a family member . . . death will come knocking. For some of us, these knocks may be overwhelming. I know because I have been there. I know what it's like to have to face death daily. I know what it's like to hold back my own tears when loved ones are grieving uncontrollably. I know what it's like to not have answers. I know what it's like to stand in faith with a mother who is believing in God for the healing of her child and then having to comfort her when her prayers remain unanswered and death has its way. I know what it is like to be overwhelmed, for indeed bereavement ministry is a heavy load sometimes. Yet there is joy in this ministry when a person goes from mourning to acceptance and even joy.

Bereavement ministry can be burdensome because the weight of death and grief and the responsibility of providing comfort, glorifying God, and impacting lives is heavy. It's burdensome when we are called to eulogize a family member or close friend. It's burdensome when we struggle to contain our emotions. It is burdensome to watch another person suffer with pain. It is burdensome when the deceased reminds us of a loved one and we are forced to think about the mortality of our own family and friends.

When three people suddenly die in a car accident—a young mother, her eight-year-old daughter, and ten-year-old nephew—and as a minister you are called to stand over the casket where both mother and daughter lay together, it can be burdensome.

When a family of four is murdered and you are faced with the task of eulogizing all the members in the same service, that's burdensome. When a fire suddenly kills two little boys, when a six-year-old girl suddenly drowns while on vacation with her grandmother, and the lives of an innocent mother and her children are suddenly taken by murder, it can be burdensome.

When a promising young military man suddenly falls asleep while driving after playing an exhausting football game, crashes his car and dies . . . when we are called to provide ministry for the *suddenlies*—the long-term illnesses that result in death, unfathomable suicides, and so much more, the load becomes heavier and heavier. In twenty-five years, I have seen so much and experienced so much, and through the years, I have learned how to lighten the emotional load.

Ministry is demanding, and it is important that all ministers employ self-care practices very early in their vocation. Self-care is important for the overall state of mind of the minister and vital in the prevention of compassion fatigue and ministry burnout. According to Christina Maslach, the author of *Burnout: The Cost of Caring*, "the burnout process begins with emotional exhaustion, a feeling of being emotionally overextended and depleted. Emotional exhaustion then adversely impacts relationships with others through depersonalization, which is a negative and detached reaction."[1]

In addition, we may face compassion fatigue, which is defined

---

[1] Christina Maslach, *Burnout: The Cost of Caring* (Prentice-Hall Inc., 1982), 3, 5.

as "the physical and mental exhaustion and emotional withdrawal experienced by those who care for sick or traumatized people over an extended period of time."[2] As ministers of empathy, constantly pouring out and being present for others, we are at risk for compassion stress, and when we do not practice self-care, everyone and everything around us will be negatively affected.

The reality is that the church is the place the world turns to when life unravels, and as leaders, we can easily become inundated with all that we are faced with on a daily basis if we don't have self-care practices.

I discovered in my ministry the importance of doing something each day that brings me joy. I discovered joy and rest for my soul through my daily Bible study, prayer, and worship. I have discovered joy in my swimming routine. Swimming has become an outlet for relaxation and comfort. It is where I find safety while simultaneously being refreshed and renewed. I am able to rest my mind as I swim laps in the water. It is in these times of swimming that my mind is at peace—my mind and body are relaxed and I am one with God and the water.

In my ministry, I have discovered the importance of balance and how necessary it is for one's overall well-being. How are you balancing life and ministry? What brings you peace and joy? How do you prevent burnout?

It is so important that as ministers we enjoy life—family, friends,

---

2   Merriam-Webster Dictionary, "compassion fatigue," accessed November 18, 2021, https://www.merriam-webster.com/dictionary/compassion%20fatigue.

and everything that life has to offer. It is crucial that as you move forward in your ministry, you recognize the need for balance. Here are a few suggestions to help you through the burdensome aspects of bereavement ministry:

- **Staying Connected to the God of the Call**
  At this point, your first thought may be, "Well, I am a minister. I have to stay connected to God." But the fact is with all the demands of ministry, oftentimes we can confuse time spent in preparation to write a eulogy or sermon or for Bible study as quality time spent with the Lord. Our time in preparation to provide ministry should be separate from our personal time with God. Staying connected means carving out time for personal prayers, reflections, devotionals, biblical meditation, fasting, and stillness in the presence of God. It is in our personal *secret place* that we are refreshed and rejuvenated. Ministry will demand much from us and pull us in many directions, but we must be intentional about maintaining a personal connection to the God of the call.

- **Setting Boundaries**
  Jesus said, "Come to me, all you who are weary and burdened, and I will give you rest. Take my yoke upon you and learn from me, for I am gentle and humble in heart, and you will find rest for your souls. For my yoke is easy and my burden is light" (Matthew 11:28–30 NIV). While we know that Jesus was referring to the burden of the law, the call to find

rest for our souls speaks loud and clear in the text. Setting boundaries means transferring the burdens of ministry back on to God. Know your physical, emotional, spiritual, and mental limitations. Whenever you believe that you are right on the brink of exhaustion, draw the line and seek rest. Now understand that this rest is not only referring to the spiritual but also our physical rest. This means that you may need to take some days off and simply sleep. Our bodies are the temple of God, and taking care of our temples will ensure that we are physically capable of doing the work that God has called us to do. We need to rest, physically and spiritually. It is in these times of resting in God that you will be strengthened and equipped to endure the torrents and waves of unexpected deaths that come with bereavement ministry.

- **Knowing This One Is Not for You**
  Not every assignment is your assignment. You do not have to say yes to everything. We are called to be obedient, and yes, once we respond, "Here am I. Send me," we must be prepared to go wherever God calls. However, knowing this one is not for you is important for self-care. I remember not wanting to eulogize a seven-year-old boy who drowned while on a family vacation. At the time, my own son was seven years of age, and so immediately I identified with the family's grief. A major key to maintaining self-care is recognizing when you may be emotionally ill-equipped to handle the situation and

be at peace with relinquishing control.

- **Read Books and Soak with Worship Music**
A good book can take your mind in a different direction. You may have a demanding schedule, but take time to read encouraging, inspirational, uplifting books. You may not be able to get through the entire book in one sitting—or even in a week or a month—but carve out time to read books that will provide rejuvenation. Discover books that speak to your soul and bring joy to your life.

In addition, I have discovered that time soaking in God's presence while listening to beautiful worship music has soothed my soul and strengthened me in times of distress. With a quick online search, you can find wonderful soaking music that ushers you into the presence of God. Listen, sit in God's presence, and let the Divine minister to you. It is in these moments of soaking in God's presence that we are waiting in anticipation of the Lord. We are waiting for directions for our lives and ministry. We are waiting for words of peace and encouragement. We sit in the presence of God and wait on Him.

Dr. Rob Reimer, in his book *Soul Care: 7 Transformational Principles for a Healthy Soul*, emphasizes the importance of spending quality time with the Lord. He says, "The presence of God is transformational. This is why you need to spend time alone with God, developing intimacy with Him as you journey toward wholeness. God is a healer, and His presence is life-changing."[3]

- **Counseling**

    Counseling, for some people, can be somewhat of a taboo subject. However, counseling is therapeutic. It allows you to share and receive the tools needed to help you journey through some of the hardest times of life. It allows you to unload the burdens that may come along with consistently dealing with death and loss. Sometimes we unload so much of our pains and grievances on our family and friends that we miss out on sharing the blessings of life. Having a counselor provides that sacred space needed to clear the troubles of your mind and heart, which then opens up a space for the joys of life.

- **Sabbaticals**

    Rest is spiritual, and sabbaticals are necessary for our emotional, physical, and psychological well-being. Sometimes we just have to take a break from the demands of ministry and daily life. I remember the moment when I was completely fatigued and I knew that I needed to take a break. I was so depleted from ministry and all my life's responsibilities. I needed restoration. During that time, I decided to take a three-month sabbatical, and it was exactly what was needed

---

[3] Rob Reimer, *Soul Care: 7 Transformational Principles for a Healthy Soul* (Carpenter's Son Publishing, 2016) 40.

for my soul to be restored. But here's the thing that I didn't know at that time: The year following my sabbatical, the world would be dealing with a major pandemic. I truly believe that this time of rest prepared me for what was to come.

Whether it's a one-month, three-month, or a year-long sabbatical, take the necessary break to be renewed, refreshed, and refueled in the presence of the Lord. Here's another thing I want to emphasize: Don't wait for that point of burnout before you decide to take a sabbatical. If possible, make it a practice to incorporate a sabbatical for at least a month every few years.

Studying God's Word and partaking in prayer, praise and worship, sabbaticals, and resting in God's presence are all spiritual disciplines that allow us to have divine, restorative encounters with God. These are but a few suggestions to help lift the load of bereavement ministry. I cannot overstress the importance of being careful not to hurt ourselves while healing others. I cannot overstress the importance of proper rest, making God top priority, and finding personal enjoyment in life. Bereavement ministry, if not balanced with self-care, will take everything from you. But when managed well, you will find that—while it may be burdensome—there is also so much joy.

I can't say how many times it has brought me joy to see someone who was so deeply impacted by grief begin to live again. The reality is that death sometimes has the tendency to take the joy out of living and dim the light of the deceased's loved ones. It is as if the grieving person dies alongside the deceased and life no longer seems worth living. But there is so much joy when I witness the power and the love of the Resurrected One as God raises them out of their grave of grief and puts joy deep down in their souls. There is joy in bereavement.

There is joy when someone tells me their personal story of how God comforted them through their grieving process. It brings joy to my soul when I know the person has moved into a place of acceptance—when I know that although they are grieving, they are grieving with hope. It brings me joy when the brokenhearted can smile and laugh and have fun again. There is joy in ministering to a room filled with unbelievers. There is joy in witnessing how, as they listen to the blessed Word of God and God moves on their hearts, at times they even surrender their lives to our Lord and Savior.

It brings me joy when families move from pain to purpose like Melinda Murray, a mother who started a foundation after losing her son suddenly to cardiac arrest while he was practicing on his college basketball court. The Dominic A. Murray 21 Foundation provides programs committed to expanding access to free and affordable heart screenings, CPR-AED training, and life-saving AED devices in under-served communities. It brings me joy to witness how this mother turned her pain into purpose so that others would not have to experience her grief.

This mother, after ten years of advocating for the health and well-being of children, was even able to get a law passed. New York's Governor, Kathy Hochul signed Dominic's Law on October 25, 2021.

Dominic's Law requires all public and non-public schools train their teaching and athletic staff and provide information to students and their families about sudden cardiac arrest; SCA signs, symptoms, risks and prevention. Melinda Murray fought for more than a decade to protect the hearts of children of New York State, and now countless lives will be saved because of Dominic's Law.

There is joy in being used by God to bring hope, to be a beacon of light. There is joy in knowing that God has given me a word for God's people that will impact their lives. There is joy in sowing seeds of faith in the midst of grief. There is joy in witnessing how God turns the pain and makes it work for good. There is joy in witnessing to unbelievers and seeing how the trajectory of their lives changes by the power of the Word. There are innumerable joys in bereavement care.

Dear minister, remember the joys of the call. If God has called you, God will sustain you. God is in the midst of us desiring to comfort God's children. Remember, we can do nothing without the Lord. It is your connection to the True Vine that equips you for the call. It is the power, strength, and grace of our savior, Jesus Christ, that endows us with the gifts and abilities to minister to the bereaved. The call is indeed a burdensome joy, but you can do all things through Christ who strengthens you. Stay the course, be faithful in the call, laugh, cry, rest, and watch God work through you. You are called, equipped, and anointed for this.

Chapter 2

DEFINE EULOGY AND PRE-EULOGY PREPARATION

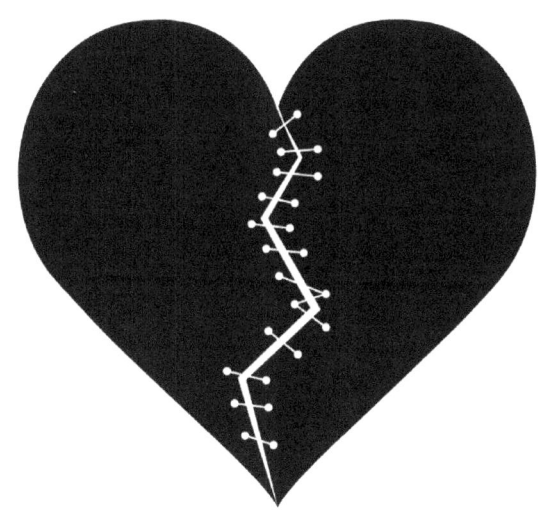

DEFINE EULOGY AND PRE-EULOGY PREPARATION

"What you leave behind is not what is engraved on stone monuments, but what is woven into the lives of others." ~ Pericles

"Eulogy
[ˈyo͞oləjē]
noun,

A speech or piece of writing that praises someone or something highly, typically someone who has just died."[4]

Merriam-Webster includes this information about eulogies:

While eulogy is also commonly found referring to words about the deceased, its basic meaning, both in English and in the Greek language from which it was borrowed, is "praise." Formed from the Greek roots eu "good" and logos "speech," a eulogy is an encomium given for one who is either living or dead. If you are praising your partner's unsurpassed beauty or commending the virtues of the deceased at a funeral, you are delivering a eulogy. With its -logy ending, eulogy means literally something like "good speech." We are told to speak only good of the dead, but a eulogist actually makes a speech in the dead person's honor.[5]

---

4   *Oxford American Desk Dictionary & Thesaurus*, 3rd ed. (Oxford: Oxford University Press, 2010), s.v. "eulogy."
5   *Merriam-Webster Dictionary*, "eulogy," accessed September 25, 2024, https://www.merriam-webster.com/dictionary/eulogy.

LENGTH OF EULOGY:

The length of a typical eulogy is approximately 15-20 minutes. It has been my experience that the family of the deceased is usually exasperated—some from traveling afar, some from funeral preparation, and some from the overall grieving process—and so delivering a eulogy beyond that time frame will only serve to cause frustration and inattentiveness. With that said, it is important to note that if the deceased is a dignitary, then the eulogy may be much longer than usual.

START WITH TIME WITH THE FAMILY:

The very first pre-eulogy step is meeting with the family. The family is the source of everything we need to know about the deceased. As eulogists, our top priority is to gain as much information about the deceased as possible in order to present a personalized eulogy. Personalization is key; I have witnessed bereaved family members bent over in grief during the service, but once I began to talk about their deceased loved ones, they perked straight up, smiled, and even laughed. It's so amazing watching the most despairing faces transform when their loved one is honorably mentioned.

Personalization is important, and while some of you may be tempted to use the obituary as your source, the reality is that there is no greater source than the family members themselves. Time with the family means discussing the life of their loved one, but it first begins with prayer. Prior to discussing any funeral details or getting any information about the deceased, it is compulsory that you pray with the family. The family needs the outpouring of the Holy Spirit in the midst of their heartache.

It is important to note that your initial meeting with the family may take up to an hour. Why? Simply because the sting of death is painful and it can become very difficult for the emotional family to speak about their loved one. Journey with them patiently and empathetically in this process. This is pastoral care in the midst. We must allow the family to express themselves and allow them to pour out their emotions in a safe and confidential environment. After you have spent some time casually talking with the family, there are some key questions to ask that will help you personalize your eulogy. Some of these questions may include:

- What type of a father, mother, sibling, or child was the deceased?
- Was he or she strict?
- Was he or she loquacious or quiet?
- What were their favorite television shows?
- What words of wisdom did the person give you while growing up?
- What were some of their favorite sayings or songs?
- Did they like to cook, and what were some of their favorite dishes?

- What were their hobbies?
- Did they like to dress up (fashionable)?
- Did they like to travel?
- Did they talk about the Lord?
- Was your loved one sick for a long time or was this a sudden death? This question is particularly important because while there are times a family may not want to disclose how their loved one died, the fact is we may need to know for safety purposes. For instance, if the deceased was murdered by a gang or if the murderer has not been captured, we may seek police protection especially for the family and ourselves. If the family is reluctant to say, do not hesitate to do some research on your own. There have been times when I have had to check the news.

Once you have collected all the information that you need, the next step is to hear from God. Prayer is essential when preparing a eulogy. You want to hear, "Thus says the Lord." God's Word will not return void. Not only are you preaching to the brokenhearted but also to the unbeliever, the atheist, and people of other religions who may very well be present at the funeral. Remember, during a funeral service, we are eulogists and evangelists all at the same time. Prayer will birth a eulogy that can deliver people out of their sins and soothe the brokenhearted.

DEFINE EULOGY AND PRE-EULOGY PREPARATION

ELEMENTS OF A GOOD EULOGY:

- Honoring the deceased—This is where the information that was collected becomes useful.
- Lifting up God's Word—The sustaining Word of God will carry family and friends not only through that day but also through the days and months ahead. It is the Word of God that brings hope and shines light into dark, grieving souls. It is the Word that ministers and draws unbelievers to Christ.

God's voice speaks through our eulogies to comfort the bereaved. While I have provided guidelines, each eulogy will be uniquely crafted. Praying, being led by the Holy Spirit, personalizing, and lifting God's Word will birth a eulogy that oftentimes becomes a beautiful keepsake that remains in the hearts of loved ones.

In the following chapters, I have shared some of the eulogies that I have prepared over the years for children, women, men, and the elderly. Each eulogy begins with a synopsis and is then broken into sections to highlight how I structured it. Use these sections as a guide to help you think about how you can possibly develop a unique eulogy. As you read these eulogies, it is my prayer that you will be inspired, informed, and equipped to provide comfort to the brokenhearted.

Chapter 3

CHILDREN

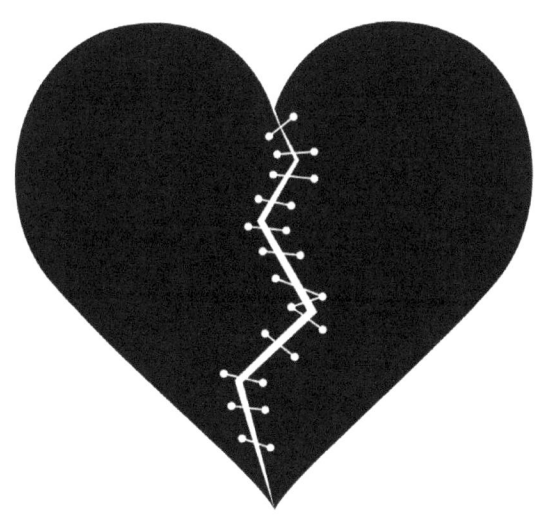

CHILDREN

Ministering to the family of a deceased child is one of the most difficult tasks one will ever face. Over the years, I have witnessed the heart-wrenching grief that mothers, fathers, and loved ones have had to endure. Whether it was a sudden death, sickness, or some other tragedy, it is never an easy task. Why? Because the child did not have an opportunity to live out his or her earthly life. Because no parent expects to bury their child. The grief is so intense, a pain that rocks the very core of a human being. But as ministers, we are empowered by the Holy Spirit to provide comfort and hope. With that said, when you spend time with the family, it is imperative that you avoid cliches like, "God doesn't make mistakes" or "God needed an angel in heaven." Simply listen with an empathetic ear, offer much needed grief counseling, and journey with them.

As you prepare to eulogize a deceased child, regardless of his or her age, personalization will honor the child and uplift the hearts of the bereaved. You can personalize the eulogy by asking for specific details about the child. Ask about their favorite food, toys, TV shows, sports, and hobbies. Ask for a description: Were they talkative, quiet, aggressive, or passive? Were they an extrovert or introvert? Gather as much information as possible. Get to know the child through the eyes and heart of the parents and loved ones. Below I have provided some of my personal eulogies as guidance. Read through them and notice how personalization and the lifted Word work together to minister, comfort, and evangelize.

EULOGY 1

Jaden Kharell King

Synopsis:
Jaden was only ten months old when he passed away. The concept for this eulogy was developed after a conversation with Jaden's aunt, who had a vision of baby Jaden in heaven. This shows why spending time with the family is important because sometimes the idea for the eulogy is divinely imparted through the conversations.

Scripture: Acts 7:56 (NIV)
"'Look,' he said, 'I see heaven open and the Son of Man standing at the right hand of God.'"

Title:
"Heaven's Happy Baby"

Section I: You don't have to start your eulogy with the Scripture, but in this case, I was led to begin with it for context. This eventually allowed me to easily transition into section II.

> *Acts 7:54-60 is a particularly sad Scripture, yet so powerful. It is sad because we see the death of a wise, godly man named Stephen. It is powerful because God granted Stephen a glimpse into heaven before he died.*

CHILDREN

Stephen had preached the truth about Jesus Christ and the reason for Christ's coming, yet he was persecuted for telling the truth. In response to his proclamations, the people became infuriated and gnashed their teeth at him. "But Stephen, full of the Holy Spirit, looked up to heaven and saw the glory of God, and Jesus standing at the right hand of God. 'Look,' he said, 'I see heaven open and the Son of Man standing at the right hand of God'" (vv. 55–56 NIV).

His persecutors did not believe anything he was saying and stoned him to death. Stephen ended his life forgiving his enemies. While they were stoning him, Stephen "fell on his knees and cried out, 'Lord, do not hold this sin against them.' When he had said this, he fell asleep" (v. 60 NIV).

Section II: In this next section of this eulogy, I began to tie Jaden's aunt's story to the story of Stephen. This connected the text to the family's experience. Now, the family that you may be working with may not have had a dramatic vision like Jaden's aunt, but the goal, as you are preparing, is to always connect the biblical text to the life and/or family of the deceased.

This story in the Bible is so similar to the experience Jaden's aunt had while Jaden was hospitalized. His aunt had a vision of Jesus standing up holding baby

Jaden in His arms. Jaden had a beautiful smile as he was looking down from heaven upon his aunt. At the same time that the vision was taking place, amazingly God had received Jaden into heaven.

God has a way of comforting us in our losses. Jaden's aunt, like Stephen, received a glimpse into eternity. This glimpse comforts us as it confirms that Jaden now has a new life in Christ, a life that is much better than the life we are living here on earth.

Section III: The next section highlights our earthly journey versus our heavenly journey. There is a deliberate and direct contrast between heaven and earth to help the listeners grasp the realities of the beauty of heaven.

Our lives on this earth are like a roller coaster—some days we are coasting up, some days we are at our peak, and some days we are going down. Our lives here are like the Ecclesiastes writer says, "There is a time for everything, and a season for every activity under the heavens" (Ecclesiastes 3:1 NIV). On this earth, we still have to face sorrow, pain, disappointments, bad days, good days, tears, and laughter.

The experiences we will still have to face here under heaven are extreme. There is "a time to be born and a time to die" (Ecclesiastes 3:2 NIV). That's extreme!

CHILDREN

But in heaven, we have a new life, and we cannot die. Under heaven, there is "a time to weep and a time to laugh" (Ecclesiastes 3:4 NIV). But in heaven, God wipes every tear away and there is no more sorrow, only joy. Under heaven, there is "a time to embrace and a time to refrain from embracing" (Ecclesiastes 3:5 NIV). Under heaven, death separates us from our loved ones, and though we would love to hold them, we must endure a time of refraining from embracing. But in heaven, we will never be separated from each other again. Under heaven, we walk by faith. But in heaven, we walk by sight. Under heaven, children are raised by their earthly parents. In heaven, children are raised by their heavenly Father.

Section IV: At this part of the eulogy, I began to talk about God's heart for children. No one wants to bury their child. Ideally all parents want to die before their children, but we know that that's not how life works. The loss of a child is a pain that cuts deep, and so reminding the family and friends that their child is precious to God helps in the healing process.

Children are very precious to the Lord. The Bible says in Matthew 21:16 (NIV), "From the lips of children and infants you, Lord have called forth your praise." Children, even little infants, do not need a worship leader. Just turn on the music and they are clapping their hands and dancing to the music. In addition, according to Psalm 8:2, the praise of children is so powerful that they silence the foe and the avenger. That is why little Jaden loved Christian music so much; God's hands were upon him.

God loves children. They are precious to God's heart. In Luke 18:15–17, parents brought their infants to Jesus so that He might touch them; but when the disciples saw it, they sternly ordered them to stop. When Jesus saw His disciples' reaction, he said, "Let the little children come to me, and do not hinder them, for the kingdom of God belongs to such as these. Truly, I tell you, anyone who will not receive the kingdom of God like a little child will never enter it" (vv. 16–17 NIV). As a popular song declares, "Jesus loves the little children, all the children of the world. Red or yellow, black or white, Jesus loves the little children of the world."

Jesus loves little Jaden more than we could ever imagine or think. The glimpse his aunt was given into eternity showed us that in heaven Jaden is being engulfed daily in pure love. Jaden and Jesus are now waiting for the day they will see you again face to face.

Section V: This is the point at which I used the information gathered from loved ones to add a personal touch to the eulogy. In this section, the focus was on the characteristics and personality of baby Jaden. I made sure to highlight nicknames, strengths, and personality traits.

> *You are going to miss your little "Yo Cutie." He was such a resilient baby. Even through his sickness, he was a happy baby. Even when he had to take his shots or it was difficult to find his veins, he would bounce right back to his cheerful self.*

> *Jaden had such a lovely disposition. Everywhere he went, people fell in love with him. In his last days of his earthly life, he loved his walker. He was able to get around and have a great time moving all over the place. Now let's imagine Jaden is running all around heaven's Baby Land, and when he gets tired of running, he can run into the arms of Jesus and fall asleep on His breast.*

Section VI: In this last section, I provided my final words of comfort to strengthen the hearts of the hearers and to bring peace.

> *I believe heaven is an awesome place for a child. May you find comfort and peace in knowing Jaden is healed and having the best time ever with the Lord in heaven's baby land. Remember the glimpse into eternity you have been given through his aunt's vision and let it comfort your hearts. See Jaden, heaven's happy baby, in the arms of Jesus and smiling down on you.*

EULOGY 2

Amira Magdi E.H. Fadlalla

Synopsis:
Amira was struck by a car on Easter Sunday. She had a massive brain injury and was hospitalized for one year. Amira eventually returned home, albeit with physical disabilities. Surrounded by the tremendous love and support of her family, she lived with her disabilities until one day God called her home. It was in speaking to God about Amira's passing that I heard the Lord say, "Heaven's playground."

Scripture: Matthew 18:4 (NRSV)
"Whoever becomes humble like this child is the greatest in the kingdom of heaven."

Title:
"Heaven's Playground"

Section I: I began this eulogy by providing a context for my focused Scripture.

> *Matthew 18 begins with Jesus's disciples asking Him a question. They asked, "Who is the greatest in the kingdom of heaven?" (v. 1 NRSV). Without a direct response, Jesus calls a child over and then says, "Truly I tell you, unless you change and become like children,*

CHILDREN

you will never enter the kingdom of heaven. Whoever becomes humble like this child is the greatest in the kingdom of heaven" (vv. 4–5 NRSV).

Section II: At this point of the eulogy, I began to speak about the characteristics of children. I wanted the hearers to understand why Jesus wanted His disciples to observe a child.

Jesus often used children to communicate spiritual truths to His hearers. In this text, Jesus calls His disciples' attention towards a child. Have you ever noticed a child's ways? Most children don't sit around worrying about life; they enjoy life. Children love to have fun. They love to play, laugh, and just be kids. They tell you they love you without reservation. They are affectionate little people—always willing to give a kiss and a hug.

Section III: The eulogy then shifts from the overall characteristics of children to a more personalized look at Amira's life, even in the midst of her suffering. Though bedridden, Amira was a resilient child.

Amira was a special child who had to endure a lot. After her accident, she had to endure fevers and life on a ventilator. I remember one day while I was visiting her, she had to wait forty-five minutes for the nurse to find her little vein. It was so hard for me and my ministry colleague to see "our little girl" suffer. That day, it was difficult to walk out of the hospital with our heads up. But Amira had a stamina that only God could have placed in the heart of this sweet, precious child. Although she was incapacitated and living on a ventilator, she would always smile and light up like a bulb whenever we sang to her.

Section IV: Here I began to address the family's losses and grief.

Many losses came with Amira's injury. There was the loss of hearing Amira's beautiful voice again. The loss of her vibrant personality. The loss of experiencing childhood with her—watching her play and have fun. The loss of experiencing her love—she would always draw for her mom and dad. The loss of spending quality time with her—she would always spend her summer vacation with her grandparents in the Poconos. You all have experienced tremendous loss, and now more than ever before, you have to depend on, lean on, and trust God.

Amira's mother prayed fervently for her daughter's healing. We all prayed. We wanted Amira healed on this side of heaven. We know that nothing is impossible for God. He is the one who created us; surely He is capable of re-creating that which has been destroyed within our bodies.

CHILDREN

Section V: At this point, I make the transition from loss to comfort. It is here that I also introduce heaven's playground.

Even though God did not answer our prayers the way we desired, God has healed Amira. In fact, she has the ultimate healing; she has entered into the kingdom of heaven. The Scriptures tell us that to be absent from the body is to be present with the Lord (2 Corinthians 5:8). Amira is now with the Lord in heaven's playground. She is free and happy. She is healed, no longer bound. She has been set free from the cocoon of a ventilator. She has been set free from her cocoon of suffering. She is no longer bound to a body that is injured. She is totally free in the presence of the Lord.

So we celebrate in faith today that Amira is eternally home with God. Amira is in heaven's playground—she is free to see what we cannot see. She is now beholding eternity. Never will she suffer again. Today, Amira is in paradise.

So today, I exhort you to keep the faith and hold on to God. Yes, Amira will be missed tremendously. Yes, we will grieve deeply. Yes, we will question the sovereignty of God. But God wants us to have the faith and trust of a little child. As a child looks to a parent and believes everything they say, we have to look to God, our Parent, and believe what He says. Our Father says He will comfort us. He says He is the source of every mercy.

He says He will never leave us nor forsake us. God, our Father, says He will be with us. In fact, in Isaiah 43:2–3, He says, "When you go through deep waters, I will be with you. When you go through rivers of difficulty, you will not drown. When you walk through the fire of oppression, you will not be burned up; the flames will not consume you. For I am the Lord, your God, the Holy One of Israel, your Savior." (NLT)

Section VI: I ended this eulogy with final words of comfort and a reminder to Amira's loved ones that their beloved child was enjoying life in eternity, playing on heaven's playground.

We grieve, but we grieve in faith because we have hope and know that we will see Amira again, healed and whole. Hallelujah! That's why the songwriter penned these words, "When we all get to heaven, what a day of rejoicing that will be! When we all see Jesus, we'll sing and shout the victory!"[6]

The kingdom of God now belongs to our precious child.

She suffered with God on the earth, but now she reigns with God forevermore. She experienced tragedy on the earth, but now she is experiencing triumph. Her life was cut short on this earth, but now she has eternal life with

---

6 "Sing the Wonderous Love of Jesus," E.E. Hewitt, accessed September 25, 2024, https://hymnary.org/text/sing_the_wondrous_love_of_jesus_sing_his.

CHILDREN

God. I guess Amira would say to us today, "Don't feel sorry for me because I trusted God and now I'm running and jumping in heaven's playground."

EULOGY 3

Madison Thomas

Synopsis: Madison passed away tragically at eleven years of age.

Scripture: 2 Kings 5:3 (NKJV)
Then she said to her mistress, "If only my master were with the prophet who is in Samaria! For he would heal him of his leprosy."

Title:
"Listen to the Voice of a Child"

Section I: I began this eulogy with the historical context of this Scripture. It was important to provide the context to reveal what God had placed on my heart about these young girls (Madison and the girl in the text). As I read the Scripture, it dawned on me that both young girls had the courage to speak out and see transformation in the lives of others. I wanted the people in attendance to hear the voice of Madison, even in the midst of their grief.

> *In our focus text for today, we find a commander by the name of Naaman. He was the commander of the army of Aram, and he was a valiant soldier, but he had leprosy. "Now bands of raiders from Aram had gone out and had taken captive a young girl from Israel, and she*

served Naaman's wife" (2 Kings 5:2 NIV). One day as she served her, "she said to her mistress, 'If only my master would see the prophet who is in Samaria! He would cure him of his leprosy' " (v. 3 NIV).

This story in the Bible is so awesome because it speaks of the power of a young girl's voice. The girl had insight that no adult around her had. She knew the God of Israel, and she knew undoubtedly that God was able to heal through the prophet Elisha. She knew that if her master, Naaman, got to the prophet, he would be delivered from his infirmity. We can imagine she felt such a conviction that she could not help but to speak up, and when she did, the adults listened to the voice of a child. Now, as you read on, you will discover that Naaman was indeed healed from leprosy because of this wise young girl's suggestion.

She is a young girl, and in fact, many translations state she was a "little girl." I don't know her exact age, but what I do know is that this young girl's voice was an instrument used to help someone else. Her suggestion changed a man's life. Not only was he healed from leprosy, but he professed his belief in the one and only God. Naaman was transformed physically and spiritually.

Section II: As I continued the eulogy, I began to highlight the connection between Madison's character and that of the character of the unnamed girl in the text. The reality was that they each had a voice, and they both helped to transform the lives of others.

> *As I thought of Madison, I realized that she was just as powerful in our day as this young girl in the Bible was in hers. The word of God says, "A little child will lead them" (Isaiah 11:6 NIV). Children, as much as they need their parents, are also leaders. Their faith in God is extraordinary, and their voices are powerful. They know how to comfort people like no one else. They love unconditionally, and they forgive easily. That is why Jesus admonishes us to be more like a child.*
>
> *Jesus isn't calling us to be childish, as in immature, but to be more childlike in our relationship with Him, as well as with each other. Madison teaches us the importance of adopting childlike attributes. Some of these attributes are:*

Section III: At this point, I wanted to provide some key takeaways based on Madison's character and personality. This section required a lot of time spent with the family of this child—time spent to get to know who she was. It is so important to highlight the character of a child when writing your eulogy.

CHILDREN

1. Being Approachable

Madison was known throughout her community. She was friendly and approachable. Her parents were astounded when even the local librarian called with her condolences. Everyone loved Madison and she loved everyone. She teaches us that as adults, we too need to be approachable.

2. Being Helpful

Madison knew how to help people and cheer them up with her jovial personality. Her parents mentioned how helpful Madison was. She volunteered to help other students and even spent time with the elderly at a nursing home. She had a heart to serve others and began serving at a young age. The songwriter penned these words, "If I can help somebody, then my living is not in vain." Her living was complete, even at the tender age of eleven.

There is a story of a young boy in the Bible. At the age of twelve, his parents were upset with him because he had separated himself from his family and did not travel with the caravan of family members. When they went looking for him, they found him in the temple speaking to the elders with great wisdom. He comforted his mother by telling her, "I am doing My Father's business." That young boy was Jesus. Madison, at the young age of eleven, was doing her heavenly Father's business; she was healing the sick with her love. Madison's helpful personality reminds us that we too need to serve and be a blessing to others.

3. Being a Peacemaker and Ambassador of Reconciliation

It was a few days before her death that Madison reconciled her differences with a friend. Her friend Melissa is a very pretty little girl, who actually looks very much like Madison. Melissa and Madison were like two peas in a pod. If you saw one, you saw the other. They were always together. But at the end of this school year, these best friends had a little falling out. However, a few days before this tragic event, Madison and Melissa became best friends again. Madison came home beaming because she had reconciled her differences with her friend. She was so happy that they were once again together as friends. These little girls teach us a valuable lesson today. They remind us that we don't know what tomorrow holds, but they teach us that we can be at peace if we reconcile our differences. Listen to the voice of a child.

4. Seeing Love in Tragedy

Madison wrote a beautiful poem of wisdom. It says:

"It was January, snow was falling

CHILDREN

It got deeper and deeper, then I fell down
But even though I was on the ground, I still I had love in my heart—love that I could feel all around me."

Madison knew that even when she fell, she would be engulfed in love. She would have love and feel loved. This poem speaks to us today. God is love, and in your tragedy, you can experience love in your heart and feel God's love all around. Listen to the voice of this child.

5. Being Disciplined in All Things

Madison was a disciplined child. She was determined to get as many awards as possible by the end of her school year. She was a focused child who received several awards, but there was one that was most important to her. It was the perfect attendance award. This child pressed her way to school every day in her starched uniform for four years, making sure not to miss a day, and at the end of the year, she was rewarded with the perfect attendance award. That's discipline. Oh, if we would listen to the voice of a child.

6. Being a Spiritual Person

Madison loved the Lord, and she loved singing the song "This Little Light of Mine." She loved Sunday school. She knew Jesus and had a hunger for God. When Madison found out about the camp's Bible study, she brought the consent papers home for her parents to fill out. Instead of choosing to sleep, play, or watch television after camp, this little girl chose to go to Bible study. Madison is speaking to us today. She is telling us to love God. She is telling us to pursue God. Listen to the voice of a child.

7. Being Goal-Oriented

Madison had goals, and she knew how to plan to accomplish them. Although her thirteenth birthday was a couple years away, she already had a vision for her big birthday party. She wanted a "big girl" party with a DJ and all.

As I pondered this little girl's desire, my imagination went wild. Madison is going to have the best party heaven can throw. She is with God her Father and Jesus, her Savior and big brother. No, she won't have an earthly party with an earthly DJ, but she will have a heavenly party. Instead of it being a DJ, it will be Madison and Jesus. Oh, what a party! All the children in heaven will gather together to celebrate the dream of a child. The angels will be there giving the children holy roller coaster rides, and then the moment will arrive—February 16, her birthday.

Can you see it? The white chariot and white horses will

do a slow trot down the golden streets of glory. They will stop right in front of the throne room, and Madison, in her beautiful pink gown, will step down as Jesus takes her by the hand. She will bow before her heavenly Father, get in His lap, and feel His love permeate her very being. Then Jesus, her big brother forever, will take her by the hand and say, "May I have the first dance, young lady?" Madison, with beaming eyes of love and joy, will waltz with the One she loves so much on heaven's crystal floor.

Section IV: I concluded this eulogy with a reiteration of the key takeaways. This helps listeners to remember the main points.

Madison taught us so much. She accomplished so much in a short period of time, and today we are reminded to:

1. *Be approachable.*
2. *Be helpful.*
3. *Be peacemakers and ambassadors of reconciliation.*
4. *See love even in tragedy.*
5. *Be disciplined in all things.*
6. *Be spiritual.*
7. *Be goal-oriented.*

Listen to the voice of a child; they have much to say!

Chapter 4

WOMEN

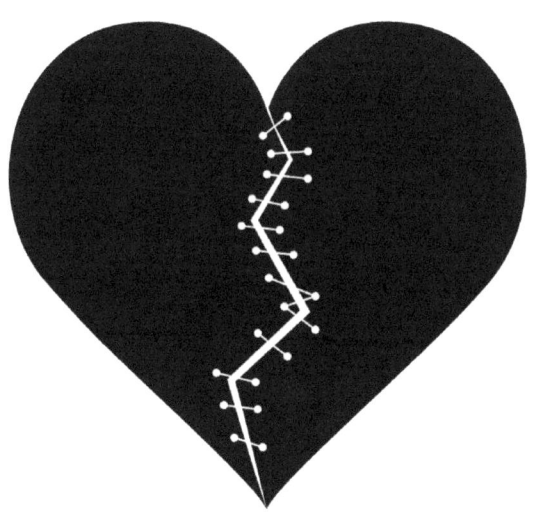

WOMEN

Mothers, sisters, aunties, good friends, wives—women from all walks of life pass away from all sorts of circumstances and illnesses. Aneurysms, cancer, heart attacks, diabetes, and various debilitating diseases have stolen the lives of great women. No one wants to bury a loved one, and women are often the matriarchs, counselors, confidantes, and even prayer warriors of our families. It is heart-wrenching when we are faced with the task of saying goodbye, but we can trust God to help the family through this difficult time. This chapter is dedicated to the women who are no longer with us but who are forever embedded in the hearts of their loved ones.

In the process of preparing a eulogy, inspiration may come in many different ways. A conversation with the individual's family is often a great source. However, when death isn't as unexpected, a discussion with the infirmed person before their demise can also be inspirational and helps to shape the overall eulogy. For instance, it was after a visit with Sister Kathy (the first eulogy in this chapter), that I received a divine download, and God gave me the Scripture. Sister Kathy passed away the following day, but the time spent in her presence provided me with the inspiration I needed to write a eulogy that honored God and spoke truth about who she was.

Let me say that it is okay to use the same Scriptures and even eulogies repeatedly. The reality is that there are some Scriptures and basic eulogies that I use on multiple occasions. "The Rock" (the third eulogy) is one of those reworked and reused eulogies and is one of my favorites.

You may or may not have the opportunity to spend time with the person you have to eulogize before their passing, but trust God always to guide you through the entire process. God will give you everything you need to minister to grieving families and friends.

EULOGY 1

Sister Kathy Jones

Synopsis: Sister Kathy passed away from a terminal illness.

Scripture: Hebrews 11:4 (NRSV)
"By faith Abel offered to God a more acceptable sacrifice than Cain's. Through this he received approval as righteous, God himself giving approval to his gifts; he died, but through his faith he still speaks."

Title:
"A Faith That Still Speaks"

Section I: Inspiration for my eulogies is often based on the faith of the men and women in the Bible. These men and women of God knew how to persevere and keep the faith despite their difficult circumstances. Kathy reminded me of the people of faith in the Word of God. She stood in the face of adversity and remained firm in her belief to the end—believing that God was faithful.

I began this eulogy by providing the context for the text. As mentioned, lifting God's Word and honoring the deceased go hand in hand. The Word of God is powerful and active. The Word of God works in the hearts of the bereaved and the hearts of sinners.

Hebrews 11 is a faith chapter that speaks of some of the great heroes of faith. The chapter begins with defining faith. It tells us that "faith is the assurance of things hoped for, the conviction of things not seen" (NRSV). In Hebrews 11:3, it states that "by faith we understand that the worlds were prepared by the word of God, so that what is seen was made from things that are not visible" (NRSV). In other words, God called the universe into existence out of nothing. God declared that it was to be, and it was. Our God is the God who created the entire universe by His word. It is in this Creator that we put our faith.

Our faith is in the One who said, "Let there be light," and there was light. Our faith is in our God who said, "Let there be a dome in the midst of the waters, and let it separate the waters from the waters" (Genesis 1:6 NRSV) and it was so. Our faith is in our God that spoke and said, "Let us make humankind in our image, according to our likeness" (Genesis 1:26 NRSV) and it was so. Elohim created us to put our faith in God.

It is in Hebrews 11 that we find many people of faith, people who believed in God. It is here we discover Abraham's great faith. It is here that the writer reminds us that it was by faith that Abraham left his home to go to a foreign land to receive his promise. "By faith he received the power of procreation, even though he was too old—and Sarah herself was barren" (v. 11 NRSV). By faith, Abraham was put to the test and offered up Isaac to God. Abraham lived life by faith, and there were many more people—such as Gideon, Barak, Samson, David, and Samuel—"who through faith conquered kingdoms, administered justice, obtained promises, shut the mouths of lions, quenched raging fire, escaped the edge of the sword, won strength out of weakness, became mighty in war and put foreign armies to flight" (vv. 33–34 NRSV).

But listen, faith also has another side to it. Hebrews 11 states that there were other people of faith who were "tortured, refusing to accept release, in order to obtain a better resurrection. Others suffered mocking and flogging and even chains of imprisonment" (vv. 35–36 NRSV). They were persecuted for their faith in God, yet they kept the faith.

Abel was a righteous man—a man of faith—and yet he was killed by his brother Cain. Abel died, but the Bible tells us that even after death his faith still speaks. Abel's faith continues to speak to us.

Section II: The eulogy then transitions from expounding on faith to connecting Kathy's faith to the biblical text. This was important because I wanted to highlight to her bereaved family and friends how Kathy's faith will always remain in their hearts, even after her death. When you are preparing the eulogy, the Holy Spirit will guide you, and much like He gave me this connection, He will open your eyes to see how the Word of God speaks to the life of the deceased.

> *In these past years, I have met some beautiful men and women of faith. They have been afflicted with severe diseases but have maintained hope and a determination to live by faith. They did not give up on God. They wrestled against sickness, principalities, and rulers of darkness, but they kept the faith. As I sat with Sister Kathy Jones last Monday, she, like the others, said these words to me: "I have faith that God is going to heal me."*
>
> *Some may say that people who are severely ill and still speak of faith are in denial—that they are fearful of facing death. But I choose to differ. I believe that their faith in God, God's Word, and what God has done for others are the reasons for their unrelenting trust and belief. They know that God has a plan and a future for them. They know that it is a future to prosper them and not harm them. They know that despite their circumstances, God will preserve their soul from all evil. They know that the Lord loves them dearly. They know that their promise from God will be fulfilled.*
>
> *As I spent time with Sister Kathy, I could tell she spent time in the face of God. God places His hand upon*

infirmed Christians who spend time in His presence. God graces them with faith. God puts a conviction within their spirit that everything is going to be alright. They have a peace that surpasses all understanding.

That is why a God-pursuing Christian who has been very ill can look you straight in the eyes and say, "I believe God is going to heal me." They know God as the Faithful One. They know God to be a healer of all infirmities. Sister Kathy knew God.

The Bible says that it is impossible to please God without faith, and Sister Kathy Jones was a God-pleaser. The Word of God says we walk by faith and not by sight. Sister Kathy Jones walked by faith. The Bible says the righteous shall live by faith, and we know that Sister Kathy Jones lived by faith.

Sister Jones knew how to worship God in her wilderness experience. On Monday, during my visit to her home, we spent time just praising God. We praised God for who God was in her life. Sister Jones went from praise to worship. The Father seeks those who will worship Him in spirit and truth. God is looking for people that will love Him in spite of their situation. God is looking for people who will know Him and love God for who He is and not just for what He can do for them. God is looking for some Kathy Joneses who have a faith that

> *will speak after they have left this earth.*
>
> *During Communion, Sister Kathy blessed God for His broken body and blessed God for His blood that was shed for us. We worshiped God with love songs. There was a sweet, sweet spirit in that house that day. What a way to spend her last day on earth—praising and singing songs to God's glorious name.*

Section III: The final section of the eulogy further highlights the faith of Sister Jones. I wanted all in attendance to grab hold of the faith that she had in God. I wanted them to leave with hope and a stronger faith in the Lord. I concluded this eulogy with praise songs—songs that invite the bereaved to praise God despite their pain.

> *Sister Kathy's faith still speaks to us today. We all know her as a woman of faith because she believed in God. Yes, we wanted a miracle on this side of heaven. We wanted God to cleanse her of her infirmity right here on earth. Yet God chose to bring her to a place where she will never have a care again in life. There will be no more sorrow for Sister Jones. God chose to bring her into a kingdom with no more sickness, no more pain, and no more death.*
>
> *God chose to bring her into His very presence, where she can now worship God face-to-face. God decided to bring*

her into the holy of holies forever. That is why we are people who grieve, but we grieve with hope.

Sister Kathy is commended today for her faith. No, she wasn't in denial, but she believed God because of God's faithfulness. She had a faith that will still speak. In your midnight hour, when all your family and friends have departed, cry out to God—the God that Sister Kathy cried out to.

Her faith still speaks. When things are not going the way you would hope them to go, sing "My Faith Looks Up to Thee." When you feel you can't make it, sing, "We've Come This Far by Faith." When sorrow overwhelms you, remember Sister Jones, a woman of faith, who kept the faith, "a faith that still speaks."

EULOGY 2

Cynthia Arno

Synopsis: Cynthia was the picture of health. She was only forty-four years of age when she unexpectedly passed away. Cynthia transitioned the evening she received her Master of Arts with honors.

Scripture: Isaiah 43:2-3a (NLT)
"When you go through deep waters, I will be with you. When you go through rivers of difficulty, you will not drown. When you walk through the fire of oppression, you will not be burned up; the flames will not consume you. For I am the Lord, your God, the Holy One of Israel, your Savior."

Title:
"Order My Steps in Your Word"

Section I: I began this eulogy by simply talking about Cynthia. Hearts were so heavy, and I believed that reminiscing about her vivacious personality would bring some comfort. In the years that I have had the honor of ministering to the bereaved, I have come to realize that talking about the personality, quirks, love, and life of the deceased often brings a smile and laughter to the hearts of family and friends. When preparing the eulogy, if led, it is okay to start with the life of the individual. Cynthia's family perked up and began to smile once I began to speak about her.

> *If you had the great opportunity to meet Cynthia Arno, it wouldn't be long before you would know that she was a singer. This woman could sing the heavens open and the Holy Ghost would fall all over you. She was God's songbird. Today, I believe she is shaking the heavens with her vibrant heart of worship before the Lord. The angels had to move over when Cynthia Arno entered the heavenly gates of glory.*

Section II: It is at this point of the eulogy I introduced the listeners to the idea of God ordering our steps and reminded them that Cynthia's steps were ordered by the Lord.

> *We don't know the time nor the hour that we will leave our earthly bodies. We have absolutely no control over that. All our days are written in God's book. However, our steps can be ordered by God each and every day. But here's the thing . . . we must ask God to order our steps in His Word.*

> *Little did we know that Cynthia would spend her last day on earth with the people she loved the most, her family. What will remain in their hearts is how happy she was as she took her final photos with them. She had accomplished a goal and received her master's degree one day, and on the same day, she entered into her Master's hands. She went from earthly glory to a heavenly glory.*

It is well with Cynthia Arno, she has accomplished the highest attainment, and she cannot go any higher.

Sisters and brothers, we cannot comprehend the mind of God. His thoughts are completely different from our thoughts. His ways are far beyond anything we could imagine. One thing we do know: Cynthia's steps were blessed and ordered by the Lord. She loved the Lord deeply, and God loves her deeply. She is God's precious daughter. God has not forsaken her but has graduated her into a new dimension with Him.

Section III: The eulogy then makes a transition and begins to highlight some popular historical and biblical figures whose steps were ordered by God. These people of faith may have died at a young age, but they fulfilled God's purpose.

We may never understand why this happened at this specific time. Many would say God's timing is off. Yet when you take a look at Cynthia's life, she left an indelible mark on this earth. There are ninety-year-olds that may not leave the mark she has left in our hearts.

Many people who have walked this earth and left an indelible mark died early, and yet they fulfilled the purposes of God. People like John the Baptist, who completely committed himself to the advancement of God's kingdom. Martin Luther King Jr., whose words touched the consciousness of this nation and this world. And lest we forget, God's only begotten son, Jesus, who suffered and died at the age of thirty-three so that we could be redeemed.

Cynthia was young, but she has fulfilled God's purposes. She will go down in history, for Brooklyn College will now offer a scholarship fund in her name.

Section IV: Here, Cynthia's legacy is highlighted. All this information was gathered through time spent with the family and through my knowledge of her as one of my students.

Cynthia's name may not have been broadcast throughout the world, but she has left something wonderful with us all. She left:

- *Her steadfast faith—she was a woman who loved God and walked by faith and not by sight.*
- *Her joy—she knew how to step into a room and fill the space with joy. She had a contagious spirit. She brought smiles to faces, and you could not be around her and not feel better. Cynthia was filled with joy.*
- *Her songs of praise—she was a worshiper with a beautiful voice. Cynthia was not only a student at Brooklyn College, but she was also a student at the Allen Cathedral Bible Institute. In fact, she was*

> in a class that I taught, Acts of the Holy Spirit in the Life of the Believer and in the Life of the Church. She loved learning about the personality of the Holy Spirit, and whenever the Spirit of God would fill the room, the psalmist Cynthia Arno would usher us into the glory of God in songs of praise. She sang for the Lord, and now she is singing in God's presence.

Section V: While much of the first part of the eulogy focused on Cynthia, her personality, and legacy, it was important to provide comfort to the family and friends in attendance and to remind them about the tactics of the enemy in the midst of grief.

> Her favorite song, "Order My Steps in Your Word" became her life. Now it has to become your life, even in the midst of your sorrow. We are here because we love Cynthia and her family. Now the question arises, How can we make it through the waters of sorrow, when our hearts are so heavy—when we miss her already and are now living on memories?

> God, how can I pass through the rivers (anniversaries, birthdays, Thanksgivings, Christmases, my accomplishments and my failures) with this broken heart of mine? How am I going to make it when it feels like I am going to drown in grief? How can I survive

the rivers of tears and the streams of disappointments? How will I make it through the fire when my child, sister, mother, best friend, confidante, or encourager will not be with me? How do I deal with the attacks of the enemy, especially in my weakest moments?

The enemy of our soul has no compassion. His job is to get us to give up on God. He wants our spirits destroyed. He wants our faith destroyed. This is his opportune time to tell you, "God is not all that!" or "If He really loved you, He wouldn't let you hurt like this." The enemy plants thoughts like this in the heart of the grieving person: "God didn't have to let this happen." These are not your thoughts; there is an evil one who is right there in our garden of Gethsemane, trying to get us to give up on God. The attacks are real, but we have some promises in God's Word that help us to win the battle.

Section VI: It is at this point that the biblical text is brought in. God's promises and divine attributes are highlighted.

The Israelites needed a word of encouragement in one of their most difficult seasons. They were living in exile in Babylon—taken away from everything that they had known. They were grieving the loss of their homeland and suffering under the Babylonian empire. It is here that God calls the prophet Isaiah to comfort God's people. Isaiah 43:2–3 is a word of assurance and comfort during calamity.

The promise for the Israelites was: "When you go through deep waters, I will be with you. When you go through rivers of difficulty, you will not drown. When you walk through the fire of oppression, you will not be burned up; the flames will not consume you. For I am the Lord, your God, the Holy One of Israel, your Savior" (NLT).

Water overwhelms and fire consumes, but God's promise to us is that we will be okay. The same God who had protected the Hebrews in the past was the same God who was there for them in their captivity in Babylon.

The same God that parted the waters of the Red Sea and the Jordan River was the same God who kept and protected the three Hebrew boys—Shadrach, Meshach and Abednego—in the fiery furnace.

If you allow God to order your steps, allow Him into your grief, then you will go through the waters, rivers, and fire a winner. You will make it to the finish line with hands raised in praise. If you allow God to order your steps, God will meet you in your troubled waters; He will be your life jacket in the currents of life. The God of the universe is with you.

God is such a mighty God that if you find it difficult to

pass through the waters of grief and sorrow, God will part them for you. God is such a powerful God that if you have to go through the fire, God will get in there with you and you shall come forth as pure gold.

God is immutable—the God who cannot change. God is the same yesterday, today, and forever. You may be grieving, but just look to God; lift up your eyes. Remember you are going through this—you are moving and you are coming out. You won't live here; you are passing through this grief. God, in His miraculous resurrection power, knows how to bring you out.

The same God that brought His Son out of the grave will bring you out of your wailing waters. We are people who put our trust in God. We will grieve, but we grieve with hope. We are not a hopeless people. We may be downcast, we may be persecuted, we may be oppressed, but we are not forsaken nor are we abandoned.

Section VII: This eulogy concluded with us revisiting the thematic Scripture and singing Cynthia's favorite song, "Order My Steps in His Word." When using a song's title as the title for your eulogy, having someone sing the song is oftentimes a powerful way to end. It invites all to sing in honor and in memory of their loved ones. If no one is available to sing, then do not hesitate to play the song using an electronic device.

"When you go through deep waters, I will be with you. When you go through rivers of difficulty, you will not drown. When you walk through the fire of oppression, you will not be burned up; the flames will not consume you. For I am the Lord, your God, the Holy One of Israel, your Savior." (Isaiah 43:2–3 NLT)

Sing: "Order My Steps in Your Word"

EULOGY 3

Lynette Taylor

Synopsis: Lynette was a middle-aged woman when she passed.

Scripture: Psalm 61:1–3 (KJV)
"Hear my cry, O God; attend unto my prayer. From the end of the earth will I cry unto thee, when my heart is overwhelmed: lead me to the rock that is higher than I. For thou has been a shelter for me, and a strong tower from the enemy."

Title:
"The Rock"

Section I: Much like Cynthia's eulogy, I opened up this eulogy highlighting Lynette's wonderful character.

> *Losing a loved one, like Lynette, can be very painful, overwhelming, and exhausting. As you reminisce on times spent together and how she touched your hearts, it brings laughter and tears all at the same time. Laughter over the good times and tears because you will miss her presence.*
>
> *Lynette Taylor was a beautiful person with a gracious heart. She loved her three children deeply. According to Kathy, her daughter, she was a woman who disliked*

few and loved so much. She was a woman who cared for others, and she knew how to lend a helping hand to those in need.

Her love will remain in your hearts forever. There is so much power in love. The Bible says that love is stronger than death. I believe in due season, your love for Lynette will overpower your grief and you will have peace in the midst of your loss.

Section II: There is a transition here from speaking about the deceased to speaking to the emotional condition of the people. I verbalized what they might have been feeling; letting them know that you understand their grief brings comfort to their broken hearts.

Right now you are going through the emotions of grief. It is tremendous because grief is deep and troubling. Some emotions of grief are denial, abandonment, rage, anger, guilt, loneliness, pain, disappointment, distrust, and helplessness. All of which can overwhelm you. It's like trying to swim with weights on your hands and feet. The pain of grief can feel like you are in quicksand: the more you try to get out of it, the deeper you go under. It's a dark place where you can't seem to see the light. Memories and feelings of emptiness consume the soul, and it is overwhelming!

Section III: The scriptural text is now tied to the grief of Lynette's loved ones. This brings God's Word and God's power to heal the broken heart into full view—especially when family and friends can't seem to see a way out of the dark days of grief.

The psalmist in Psalm 61 was experiencing a troubling of the soul and needed to get out. He wanted God to hear his cry, but not only to hear his cry, but also to attend unto his prayer.

According to Willem A. VanGemeren, author of Expositor's Bible Commentary, it seems that the psalmist felt so far from God that he speaks to Him from a great distance. "From the end of the earth will I cry out to thee" is most likely a metaphor for despair and alienation. This person was in great distress.[7] The psalmist's heart was overwhelmed, and he needed strength, far beyond anything that he himself possessed.

We all need a source of strength that goes beyond ourselves when we lose someone so dear to our hearts. The rock is a metaphor for protection. It denotes a fortified or strategic place where one can find refuge (Psalm 27:5). The psalmist's confession of "the rock that is higher than I" expresses faith in the Lord's exalted

---

[7] Willem A. VanGemeren, *The Expositor's Bible Commentary: Psalms, Proverbs, Ecclesiastes, Song of Songs*, ed. F. E. Gaebelein (Zondervan, 1991) 5: 418.

position and His ability to deliver.[8]

When we are led to the rock, we are led to a place of safety, comfort, and refuge—a place of peace where emotions cannot overwhelm us. It is the Lord that sustains us in times of trouble. That is why the psalmist cried out to God. He asked God to attend unto his prayer. He needed to be led to God.

During praise and worship, we sang a song entitled "I Go To the Rock." This psalm, however, reminds us that there will come a time when it is so dark that you will have to be led to the rock. You have to be led to safety. You will have to be drawn out of your trouble and the hand of God will have to pull you out. The only way to get out is to be led out by the One who knows the way out.

This psalmist recognized that he couldn't get out unless God brought him out. When we face sorrow, we also must understand that it is a season in life when we must cry out to God to lead us to Him.

The psalmist also recognized that he needed to get to a place in God that was higher than his problems, higher than his fears, and higher than his disappointments. "Lead me to the rock that is higher than I." For the psalmist, the rock was a symbol of covering and shelter;

---

8   VanGemeren, *The Expositor's Bible Commentary*, 418.

the rock was a safe place, away from trouble.

Section IV: Acronyms are a great way to keep listeners engaged and often make the eulogy more memorable. Death can be traumatizing, and the brain may be overwhelmed with thoughts. Including an acronym highlights key takeaways.

The ROCK can be used as an acronym:

R *is for resting place: When we are led to God, our Rock, we will experience rest for our souls. He will make you lie down in green pastures. He will lead you beside the still waters (based on Psalm 23:2 NKJV). You will have pure and true rest in the midst of your sorrow. God gives your soul—the very core of your emotions—a resting place.*

O *is for open arms: The Rock has open arms. He is waiting right there to embrace and comfort you. God will be there for you in your midnight hour to hold you and hug you, to wrap His loving arms around you so that you can experience solace in your deepest pain. In His arms, you will experience His deep and pure love. There is nothing that can compare to the peace of God's arms.*

C *is for Care: The Rock cares for you. There is no one on earth and in heaven that can care for you more than God. King David penned these words, "How precious* *also are thy thoughts unto me, O God! How great is the sum of them! If I should count them, they are more in number than the sand" (Psalm 139:17–18 KJV). There is not a moment that you are not on the mind of God. God's Word says to cast "all your care upon Him, for He cares for you" (1 Peter 5:7 NKJV). "When my heart is overwhelmed: lead me to the rock that is higher than I."*

K *is God knows: God our Rock knows all things. God knows exactly how you feel. God knows everything about you. God knows your thoughts before you even speak them. God knows the heaviness within your heart. God knows the pain you are feeling, and in God's lovingkindness He will pour out His peace and mend your broken heart.*

Section V: The concluding section is my final opportunity to lead them to the God who upholds them during their most difficult times. It is here that I reiterate the need for us all to cry out to God, especially when our hearts are in despair.

There are going to be moments when friends and loved ones have gone back to their own homes, and the reality of losing your loved one will begin to set in. Anniversaries and holidays will bring back the good memories you shared together, and tears will flow. Grief is real, and we can't get around it; we must go through it. However, the One who is able to help you is right there for you when you cry out to God. When your heart is overwhelmed, just cry out to the Lord and the Rock will lead you out of despair.

Like the psalmist cried, cry out, "Hear my cry, O God; attend unto my prayer. From the end of the earth will I cry unto thee, when my heart is overwhelmed: lead me to the rock that is higher than I" (Psalm 61:1–2 KJV).

The Rock will bring rest. Lead me to the Rock whose arms are opened at all times. Lead me to the Rock who cares. Lead me to the Rock who has all knowledge and understanding. Lead me to the Rock!

EULOGY 4

Marie Sanchez

Synopsis: Marie was pregnant with twins when she passed.

Scripture: Hebrews 4:12 (AMPC)
"For the Word that God speaks is alive and full of power [making it active, operative, energizing, and effective]; it is sharper than any two-edged sword, penetrating to the dividing line of the breath of life (soul) and [the immortal] spirit, and of joints and marrow [of the deepest parts of our nature], exposing and sifting and analyzing and judging the very thoughts and purposes of the heart."

Title:
"God's Word Will Heal You"

Section I: This section begins with the deceased's favorite Scripture and provides some context so that the hearers may have a better understanding of the text.

> *Hebrews 4:12 was dear to Marie's heart—it was her favorite Scripture, and today I can say that it is a spiritual baton that she now leaves to you all. The book of Hebrews was written by an unknown author who wrote it to provide instructions to Jewish believers. The letter was written as an exhortation to encourage persecuted believers to continue in God's grace. In the*

> *midst of your great loss, Marie's favorite Scripture now serves as encouragement for your broken hearts.*
>
> *Losing Marie, Jacob, and Andrew has crushed your spirits. Your dreams are shattered, and the darkness of sorrow has taken over your days and nights. But God is extending God's grace in the midst of your sorrows.*

SECTION II: The next section speaks briefly about God's grace to uphold us in the midst of sorrow. I wanted hearers to know that God's Word is God's powerful grace extended to us at all times.

> *Grace is strength poured into us that is beyond our own strength. Grace is unmerited favor from the Lord. Hebrews 4:14–16 says, "Therefore, since we have a great high priest who has ascended into heaven, Jesus the Son of God, let us hold firmly to the faith we profess. For we do not have a high priest who is unable to empathize with our weaknesses, but we have one who has been tempted in every way, just as we are—yet he did not sin. Let us then approach God's throne of grace with confidence, so that we may receive mercy and find grace to help us in our time of need" (NIV). Grace is God's power to uphold us when we are weak. It is God's ability to sustain us through the most difficult trials of life. God's grace is always extended to you. God's grace is God's faithfulness to fulfill God's Word.*

SECTION III: The transition here focuses on God's Word as described in Hebrews 4:12. There is also a brief mention of an article I read. Relatable stories draw the listeners in, support the major points of the eulogy, and comfort the listeners as they realize that they are not in this sorrow by themselves.

The Word of God is powerful—it is energetically effective and successful. The power of God's Word can be seen in creation. When God said, "Let there be". . . it was. God said, "Let there be light," and there was light. God's Word is quick, and it performs mightily in the earth and in the hearts of humanity. It is a sharp weapon—it is a sword against the enemy of our souls. In the days to come, when family members have traveled back to their respective places, it will be the Word that will be active in you to sustain you and heal your broken hearts.

I was reading an article titled "Embracing the Pain" by Gerald Sittser, who had lost three family members to a car accident: his mother, wife, and child. In the deep darkness of his soul, he spent many nights in a rocking chair in anguish. He wanted to pray but had no idea what to say. Groans became his only language—a language that he knew in his heart that only God could understand. But then he remembered the Scripture in Romans 8:26–27 (KJV), "Likewise the Spirit also helpeth our infirmities: for we know not what we should pray for as we ought: but the Spirit itself maketh intercession for us with groanings which cannot be uttered. And he that searcheth the hearts knoweth what is the mind of the Spirit because he maketh intercession for the saints according to the will of God." As he pondered the text, he suddenly realized that the Holy Spirit was praying on his behalf. In the midst of deep anguish, he recognized that even though he could not utter the word, the Word was actively working in his life. Beloved, in our darkest state, God's light will enter through by the power of God's Word.

God's Word will sustain your walk through this valley of sorrow. God will be with you. The Word will heal the anguish in your souls. It will sustain your faith when you just don't have an answer. God knows the pain within your hearts. He knows your thoughts of anger, regrets, and turmoil. Hebrews 4:12 reminds us that God's Word has the power to discern what's in each of our hearts. The Word discerns thoughts and intentions. God's Word knows exactly what is going on in our souls—that is, the seat of our emotions. When we speak the Word and believe it, it will restore our souls. We need the power in God's Word to provide hope beyond the grave.

SECTION IV: It is here that I focus on the life and character of the deceased.

> *So Marie has passed the baton. She has left you with her favorite Scripture; now you grab a hold of it. Marie trusted in God's Word, and as she passes the baton, she invites you to trust it as well.*
>
> *Marie, Jacob, and Andrew are present with the Lord. Nothing can separate them from God's love. Romans 8:38 promises us that "neither death, nor life, nor angels, nor principalities, nor powers, nor things present, nor things to come, nor height, nor depth, nor any other creature, shall be able to separate us from the love of God, which is in Christ Jesus our Lord" (KJV). Death does not take away or diminish your love for your loved ones.*
>
> *You will always love Marie, and you will always have her in your hearts. You will always remember how she was full of life. She had such a joyful spirit. Marie was a go-getter. She would always say, "Don't settle just for what you are doing now; keep pushing forward." She knew how to press through the obstacles of life to accomplish her goals. She wanted the very best for her family and friends. She wanted you all to succeed in every way—not only in your careers but also in your spirituality. Marie was a phenomenal woman. You will always treasure the sweetness of her words, laughter,*

and inspiration. She was organized, energetic, a lover of trees, and a devoted wife to her husband, Richie.

Marie and Richie's marriage was a true love story that began at the age of thirteen. It was in youth that she declared, "He shall be my husband," and unbeknownst to her, this young boy also declared, "She shall be my wife." God in His sovereignty allowed true love to come together. Almost seven years of marriage, but a lifetime of love. Her last words to him were "I love you." Today, they may be separated physically, but their love will remain intact eternally.

SECTION V: I conclude with final encouragement and a reminder that it is God's Word that will heal and sustain them in the days to come.

Marie has passed the baton. In leaving you with her words of encouragement and her favorite Scripture, she is saying, "Until we see each other again, let the Word of God heal you." In the days ahead, seek God through God's Word, and allow God to work mightily in your hearts.

EULOGY 5

Julia Johnson

Synopsis: The circumstances around Julia Johnson's passing are unknown.

Scripture: John 14:1-3 (NKJV)
"Let not your heart be troubled; you believe in God, believe also in Me. In My Father's house are many mansions; if it were not so, I would have told you. I go to prepare a place for you. And if I go and prepare a place for you, I will come again and receive you to Myself; that where I am, there you may be also."

Title:
"I'm in My Father's House"

SECTION I: This eulogy begins with a focus on how Sister Johnson's selfless life and devotion to others spoke for her, even after her passing. In addition, starting a eulogy highlighting the lyrics of a song that speaks true to the deceased's character helps to provide a memorable connection for the hearers.

> *Sister Johnson lived a selfless life helping other people. She cared for the Harris family. She loved them and helped them throughout their daily lives. She was the one they could count on to escort the children back and forth*

to school. She was the one they could count on to make a delicious meal for the children. It was Sister Johnson's willingness to stay with the children that allowed their parents to take a vacation. Sister Johnson's work spoke for her.

SECTION II: Here, I transitioned from speaking about her character to speaking about her faith, which then seamlessly segued into the focused Scripture.

She was also a woman of faith. In fact, her favorite words of wisdom were, "Thank God for everything. Thank Him for the good and thank Him for the bad . . . because bad is always good." She could find the good in every situation. One has to have a relationship with Almighty God to see the good in the bad. Sister Johnson had a strong relationship with the Lord. She walked with the Lord for a long time. Much like the disciples in this biblical text, she spent time in the presence of God.

For three years, the disciples spent time in the presence of Jesus. They traveled with Him, learned from Him, and witnessed His miracle-working power. They were witnesses to miracles of healing. They watched in amazement as He calmed a raging sea, walked on water, and multiplied five loaves of bread and two fish into a feast that fed more than five thousand people. They witnessed many great things in His presence, but Jesus—this mighty man of miracles, signs, and wonders—threw a curveball.

Jesus instructed the disciples, "Let not your heart be troubled." These words would seem unusual, but He knew what they were going to experience after His crucifixion on the cross. He knew His gruesome suffering would shake their faith, and so He spoke a word into their hearts that would carry them through the storm: "Let not your heart be troubled." The promise that Jesus spoke to His disciples holds true for us today. Let not your heart be troubled.

SECTION III: Here, I wanted to not only provide key definitions, but I wanted the hearers to understand the context, which further provided insight into the text.

The Greek word for "troubled" (tarasso) means to "disturb, agitate, stir up."[9]

Let not your heart be disturbed because God has a perfect plan for His children that is eternal. Jesus spoke these words of comfort to the disciples and then He said, "In my Father's house are many mansions: if it were not so, I would have told you. I go to prepare a place for you. And if I go and prepare a place for you,

---

9   Strong's Concordance, "5015. tarassó," accessed September 25, 2024, on BibleHub https://biblehub.com/greek/5015.htm.

I will come again and receive you to Myself; that where I am, there you may be also" (John 14:2–3 NKJV).

It is important to note here how the words Jesus spoke would have been understood by His disciples because of their culture and tradition. In those days, it was customary for a son to prepare a room for his bride that was attached to his father's house. The couple would come together to announce their engagement to their families, there would be a celebration, and finally, the groom-to-be would go back to his father's home and begin the project of building another room on to his father's house. Once the room had been prepared, he would go and take his bride. The bride would never know the exact time of the groom's arrival, but once he had arrived, she would hear a loud shout in the streets announcing that the groom was ready for his bride. There would be a great celebration as he brings his bride to her new room.[10] Jesus said, "I go to prepare a place for you."

SECTION IV: The focus here is Sister Johnson's new experience in her new heavenly home. I wanted to provide

---

10 Isaac Landman, ed., *The Universal Jewish Encyclopedia: An Authoritative and Popular Presentation of Jews and Judaism Since the Earliest Times* (Universal Jewish Encyclopedia, Incorporated, 1939), 369-373.

comfort to the family while tying the text to her new life in glory.

> Sister Johnson heard the shout in the streets of glory, "The groom has arrived." She now has a wonderful everlasting life with the Lord. Jesus promised His disciples and He promised us that He is preparing a place for us. It is a place where God wipes away every tear that you ever shed. A place where God takes away every pain that you ever experienced here on earth. In this place, there is no need for hospitals. No need for medicines. No more sickness. No more doctors. It is a place where there will be no more dying. No more funerals. No more crying—for the former things are passed away. Sister Johnson has gone home to that place.
>
> We may not know the exact time Jesus is going to call us home, but we can rest assured that we have an eternal room awaiting us. There is a blessed assurance in our souls when we believe our loved one is safe in the arms of our heavenly Father. We can find rest for our souls when we know that our loved one has started a new and wonderful life in the presence of God.

SECTION V: At this point, I used my imagination to paint a picture of how Jesus would welcome Sister Johnson home.

> The Lord looked down on His daughter, Sister Johnson, and said:

> *"It is finished.*
> *You have run your course; you have fought the good fight.*
> *Come on in and receive the crown of righteousness that has been laid up for you.*
> *Come on in and see Jesus your Redeemer.*
> *Come on in and walk the streets of gold.*
> *Come on in and see the saints and loved ones who have been waiting for you.*
> *Come on in and rest from all your labor.*
> *Come on in and dwell with us.*
> *Your room has been prepared so that where I am, you may be also.*
> *Come on in and meet your heavenly Father face-to-face.*
> *Come on in and meet Jesus, your resurrected Savior.*
> *Come in, Sister Johnson, you now have a new home in my Father's house."*
> *Hallelujah!!!*

SECTION VI: The eulogy concluded with a final song, "In My Home Over There," that pulls the entire eulogy together. In addition, I ended with the thematic Scripture as a final word of encouragement.

> *Family and friends, we find comfort today in knowing Sister Johnson is filled with joy in her home over there—there in her Father's house. Today, the Lord wants you to hold on to the truth, rest in God's arms, and know that*

God will carry you through. Today, God says, "Let not your heart be troubled; you believe in God, believe also in Me. In My Father's house are many mansions; if it were not so, I would have told you. I go to prepare a place for you. And if I go and prepare a place for you, I will come again and receive you to Myself; that where I am, there you may be also" (John 14:1–3 NKJV).

Sister Johnson is in her Father's house.

Chapter 5

MEN

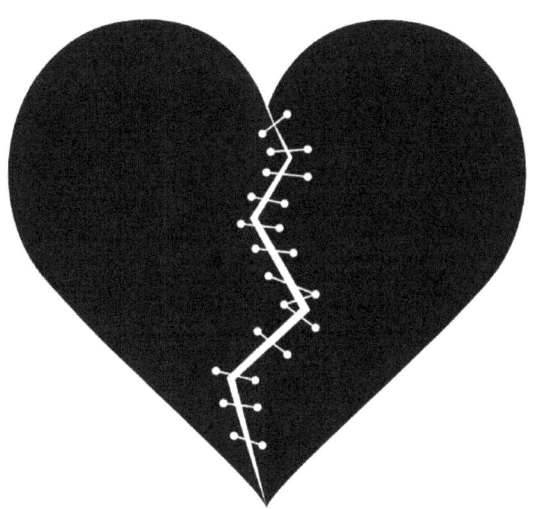

MEN

As the Director of Bereavement, I prepare an age graph of the deaths within our church. This age graph is a report that provides the church with data about all the funeral services officiated throughout the year. When we look at the graph, we are able to not only see how people passed away in that year, but we can learn about the age range of the deaths. For many years, what has astounded me was the number of men who passed away under the age of fifty. In fact, the number of male deaths younger than fifty outnumbered the deaths of males older than fifty.

I've had to eulogize men from all walks of life. I've ministered to family members who were mourning the sudden passing of the male figures in their lives: men who were murdered, men who were involved in car accidents, men who succumbed to an unhealthy lifestyle, men who passed away after battling a terminal disease—men who died from various circumstances. This chapter focuses on how to eulogize males.

EULOGY 1

Brother Edwin Brown

Synopsis: Brother Brown passed away after battling sickness.

Scripture: Jeremiah 8:22 (NIV)
*"Is there no balm in Gilead?
Is there no physician there?
Why then is there no healing
for the wound of my people?"*

Title:
"There Is a Balm in the Secret Place"

Section I: Beginning the eulogy with an illustration is a great way to connect your main point with your audience, and it makes the eulogy more relatable.

> *Recently I had a steam burn that was so painful. The only thing I could do was to place my fingers in a cup of ice water to soothe the pain. When I took my hand out of the cup, the pain would become intense within minutes. The ice water was a balm that helped to soothe the pain. We all need a soothing balm from time to time, but especially when we lose a loved one.*

MEN

God wants to soothe your grieving hearts. If you draw near to God, God will be like that ice water to my fingers. God will comfort and soothe you. God will reveal that He is the balm you can always rely on.

Section II: This is where I began speaking about the deceased. It's amazing what happens in the hearts of loved ones when we speak about the deceased. Sadness turns to smiles, and joy arises in the hearts of all.

Much like my steam-burnt fingers, one minute you may feel okay—enjoying friends, laughing—but then the next minute, you may feel the sting of grief. When you think about the years God has graced you with this wonderful man, Brother Brown, there will be so many good memories that will flash through your mind. Memories that will put a smile on your face but will also remind you of your loss.

Tears will flow for Mrs. Brown, but even in her grief, she will be comforted by memories. She was grateful to have him as her husband for forty-four precious years. With much love in her heart, she remembered his talkative personality. She spoke about his love for sports cars and travel. Her words were "We've had a good life together." What a blessing! To live with someone you enjoy. Not everyone can say, "We've had a good life together." Some couples may have stayed together for years, but they do not have that testimony. Mrs. Brown recognized that she was blessed with a good man, and she took care of him. She loved him when he was in good health, and she loved him in sickness—a woman who stood by his side all the way.

Memories will be invaluable and precious to you all. You will always treasure them in your heart, but how do you face the days to come without the presence of your loved one?

Section III: At this point, the focused text is expounded on and tied into the idea that there is a healing balm for all in God's secret place.

The Israelites in this Jeremiah text needed healing for their souls. The balm in Gilead was "an aromatic, medicinal substance derived from plants. Gilead was an area east of the Jordan River, well known for its spices and ointments. The 'balm of Gilead' was, therefore, a high-quality ointment with healing properties."[11] There was a balm in Gilead, but today, God has made available to us a balm that heals emotional wounds, physical wounds, and psychological wounds.

---

11 "What Is the Balm of Gilead?," GotQuestions.org, accessed May 16, 2016, http://www.gotquestions.org/balm-of-Gilead.html.

God's presence is our balm that soothes our grief-stricken hearts. It is in the secret place that God comforts us. The Word of God will rise up in our souls, and we will be reminded of the faithfulness of God. A song may come to you in the midnight hour that will carry you throughout the day. During these times, you will be reminded that God is your very present help in a time of need (Psalm 46:1). The Lord will show up in all kinds of ways. He will send people to bless and encourage your heart. The soothing presence of God surrounds us in the time of trouble.

God is faithful to His beloved ones. God draws close to the brokenhearted and the crushed in spirit. When no one else is around, the Lord will meet you in that quiet place. As you cast your burdens onto Him, God will sustain you. When you are weary and burdened, draw close to God and He will take you into a place of rest. It is a place where you can be revived, be refreshed, and find relief. That is God's promise—to restore our souls.

There is a secret place in God, and we have to make a decision to enter that place. It is a place of healing and recovery. It is a place that we can hear directly from God. It is a place where we can find the strength and encouragement to go on. It is a place of holiness, for it is the presence of God. It is in the secret place where we find the balm to soothe our pain. It is where we find:

Section IV: The use of an acronym enables the listeners to remember the main points of the eulogy.

> *B—Beauty for Ashes: God sees you in your distress, and God will take what seems so hopeless, like ashes, and make it into something beautiful. The most grievous season of your life will yield beauty in unexpected ways.*

> *A—Angels: God sends ministering angels to strengthen us when we are weary of the pain. You will feel a touch from heaven and know that God is with you. God's angels will strengthen you to go on.*

> *L—Liberty: God will set you free from the spirit of heaviness and despair that tries to weigh you down. Where the Spirit of the Lord is, there is freedom. The shackles of grief will be broken in the secret place.*

> *M—Mediator: The Holy Spirit is our comforter. God's Spirit will console you and fill you with peace.*

Section V: I concluded this eulogy with words of encouragement. I wanted loved ones to remember that when the service was over, they could find solace in the secret place.

> *In your time of grief, find the secret place. You don't have to have a lot of words. All you need to say is "God, here*

I am. Heal me." In God's presence is fullness of joy, and it is in God's presence that God soothes our deepest pain. Look to God each and every day, and you will find there is a balm in the secret place.

EULOGY 2: EVANGELISTIC EULOGY

Darian

Synopsis: Darian was involved in street life and was murdered. Due to his violent lifestyle, when I interviewed the family, they had very little to say about him. However, in one conversation with one of his loved ones, they expressed that in spite of how he lived his life, they remembered him as a little boy and loved him regardless. This is an evangelistic eulogy. It was a love call from God to the many unsaved attendees.

Scripture: Luke 15:20 (NIV)
"So he got up and went to his father.

"But while he was still a long way off, his father saw him and was filled with compassion for him; he ran to his son, threw his arms around him and kissed him."

Title:
"Come Home"

Section I: Sometimes the only chance we have to preach the gospel to the unsaved is at funeral services. This eulogy begins with a strong evangelistic tone. Truth be told, this eulogy was more like a complete sermon than a eulogy that speaks of the deceased. The reason was simply because, as mentioned, Darian's family had nothing good to say about him. After a conversation with his mother, I was led to write this eulogy with an evangelistic tone to point the unsaved attendees to Christ. Sometimes as ministers you will be called to eulogize a Darian, and in those cases, you may be led to simply minister to the brokenness of the living, or you may be led to steer family members and friends toward the Savior. Either way, God will lead you and you will be able to minister to the brokenhearted.

> *As I talked with Darian's mother, there was a deep concern and cry in her heart for her children. She desired deeply that they would each receive the free gift of salvation and have the joy of the Lord in their lives. This eulogy is dedicated in the name of Darian, and it is an invitation from God to you. It is an invitation to come home. Today, I invite you to hear the voice from heaven. It is the voice of God that beckons all to come home.*

Section II: With a focus on the sovereignty of God, I began by magnifying God's creative power and presence in our lives, even before we were born. As we magnify the Lord, we, as ministers, can rest assured that the Holy Spirit is working in the souls of the bereaved.

> *When we think of our earthly home, we often feel there*

is nothing like home. We can go on a wonderful vacation and see the most beautiful places or visit families in different parts of the country, but when we come home from vacation and snuggle into our beds, there is nothing like the comfort of familiarity. There is nothing like home. But did you know that before we were created in these bodies, we had a home?

Before we were born in these bodies, our spirit was home with God. We were in Him and God was in us, and it was God's love for us that made Him decide to make a body for us to live in. How do we know this to be true? God said to Jeremiah the prophet, "Before I formed you in the womb I knew you" (Jeremiah 1:5 NKJV).

Psalm 139 states that God is awesome and God knows everything about us. God knows our thoughts before we even speak them. God knows our every move. God knows when we sit and when we rise. Verses 15–16 says, "My frame was not hidden from You When I was made in secret . . . Your eyes saw my substance, being yet unformed" (NKJV). This means that before we were even formed in the womb, God saw us and approved us.

We are eternal beings. God told Jeremiah that "before you were born I sanctified you" (Jeremiah 1:5 NKJV). I want you to know that God is greater than the years we live here on earth. God is eternal, and we were made

> *to be eternal. Our eternity began before we were even knitted together in our mothers' wombs.*
>
> *The difference between living beings, such as animals, and us is that God breathed the breath of life in Adam and made all humans in God's image. The Bible states in Genesis 1:26, "God said, Let Us make man in Our image" (NKJV).*

Section III: Here I wanted to focus on what it means to be made in the image of God.

> *What is it to be made in the image of God? We are to be a reflection of God. So, when God made us, it was His intention that we would carry the same characteristics of God. God is holy, and God calls us to be holy. To be holy means to be set apart, to not reflect the ways of the world but to reflect God's love, faithfulness, kindness—God's very nature.*
>
> *We were created to glorify God. If we do not glorify God, we are not living the life God planned for us. When we don't glorify God with our lives, we are living a life below our divine purpose. God's plan for us is to give us a future and a hope. God's plan is all good. God has a plan for us while we journey on this earth.*

Section IV: At this point, I began to expound on the biblical text about the prodigal son. I was very intentional about telling the story so that the unsaved attendees would not only have a clear understanding about the events of the text but will have an emotional connection to the text.

When God says, "Come home," He is beckoning us to come to a place that we had in Him before we were even born. Home for us is with God. If you are not with God, you are not home. Home in God is prosperity of the soul. Home is a place of love and peace in God. Home is a place where you can cast all your cares on Father God, and He shall sustain you. Home in God is right here on earth. If you come home, God throws the biggest party for you. God celebrates you when you come home.

The story in Luke 15 reveals to us how our heavenly Father responds when we come back home to live with Him. The story is about a son that was home with his father but decided he wanted to leave home and have some fun out there in the world. He was supposed to receive this inheritance after his father's death. However, the son asked his father for his inheritance while his father was alive. The father gave his son his inheritance, and the son left home and set out on his journey. Without the guidance of his father, he squandered all his wealth and was left with nothing. He became so poor that he ended up eating the same food that the pigs ate. One day, the young man came to himself and said, "I am better

> *off going back home than to wallow in a pig's pen." He said, "I will arise and go to my father, and will say to him, 'Father, I have sinned against heaven and before you, and I am no longer worthy to be called your son. Make me like one of your hired servants"* (Luke 15:18–19 NKJV).

> *The father was so elated that his son had come home that he threw the biggest party ever for him. The father told his servants to "bring out the best robe and put it on him, and put a ring on his hand and sandals on his feet" (v. 22 NKJV). He said in verse 23, "Bring the fatted calf here and kill it. Let us eat and be merry" (NKJV).*

Section V: At this point in the eulogy, I transitioned to include personal application—connecting the text to the lives of the attendees.

> *Our heavenly Father feels the same way toward us when we come home. Living without Him may at times seem fun, unrestrictive, and pleasurable, but in the end, life apart from God leads to destruction, loneliness, and pain. When we come to our senses and realize that the best place to live is with God and in God's presence, God then throws a party in heaven. The angels rejoice when one of us decides to come back home. When we say to ourselves, "I am going back to my Father; I can't live like this another day," God hears our cry and is right*

there to receive us. There is a voice from heaven, and it is the voice of the Father beckoning us to come home.

What I love about this story is the eagerness of the father in verse 20. The text tells us that the son "arose and came to his father. But when he was still a great way off, his father saw him and had compassion, and ran and fell on his neck and kissed him" (NKJV). That father never stopped looking for his son to return home. This is the love of our heavenly Father. God is compassionate, filled with grace, and is eager to have one of His children return home.

Section VI: I concluded this evangelistic eulogy with an invitation to salvation. This type of eulogy is focused on the love of God and the desire for God's children to come home.

God's love for you is so strong, and He longs for you to come home. God will not force you to return to Him—it has to be your decision. In spite of your shortcomings, God desires to have you back.

The father in the story spoke these words: "We had to celebrate and be glad . . . [he] was dead and is alive again; he was lost and is found" (v. 32 NIV). We are lost without God, but when we come home, we will find life. God is speaking to you. He has heard the cry of Darian's mother's heart—a cry for her children to be saved. Now, God your Father is looking for you to come home.

Family, friends, loved ones, no one knows the day or the hour that we shall leave this earth. We cannot control the day we are born, and we cannot control the day we die. However, we can determine in our hearts to live at home with the Father. The Father loves you and is calling your name. God says, "My son, come home. My daughter, come home." There is a heavenly host waiting to celebrate when you come home.

EULOGY 3

Devonte Smith

Synopsis: Devonte was about thirty-two years of age the day that I met him. I remember so clearly walking into his hospital room, where his beautiful wife and father stood by his side. They had just found out that Devonte had a brain tumor. After a two-year battle, Devonte passed away.

Scripture: Psalm 139:16 NLT
"You saw me before I was born.
Every day of my life was recorded in your book.
Every moment was laid out
before a single day had passed."

Title:
"My Son Devonte"

Section 1: Assembled were people from all walks of life, faiths, doubts, and unbeliefs. I wanted to speak truth, in love, to their hearts. I began this eulogy with a focus on God's infinite wisdom and knowledge.

> *Psalm 139 was written by King David, and it is a beautiful description of how intricately God knows each and every one of us. God takes a personal interest in each and every day of our lives.*

God knows everything about us. He knows us better than we know ourselves. God knows every word that will proceed from our mouths before we even speak. He knows every thought that is not spoken. He knows when we stand and when we sit. God goes deep within the heart—to places no one else can enter. He is the healer of broken hearts, the restorer of crushed souls.

This psalm reminds us that both our physical and emotional natures result from God's creative activity. The entire process of life from conception onward occurs through God's creative power and wisdom. God knows everything about us.

Psalm 139 reminds us that one cannot escape the presence of God. Every place is accessible to God, even the deepest depths of the dead's abode. David declared in this psalm, "I can never escape from your Spirit; I can never get away from your presence. If I go up to heaven, you are there. If I go down to the grave, you are there" (vv. 7–8 NLT).

Section II: At this point, I wanted to remind all in attendance that God orchestrated the events of Devonte's life.

God knew all the days of Devonte's life. They were all written in God's book. God knew that he would be loved by many. God knew that Devonte's princely charm would light up every path he took. God knew that Devonte would be a man of character—one who made others proud.

God has always been intimately involved in Devonte's life. God handpicked his loving mother and father. God knew about the little brother that he would adore. It was God who led him to a specific college to meet a specific woman who would become his anointed and faithful wife.

It was God who strategically placed the right people in his life for the purpose of helping God's son Devonte over what he used to call the "speed bumps" of life. God has never forsaken Devonte.

Section III: The transition here led me to compare Devonte's life to other notable men who lived a short life of purpose.

His journey on earth may not have been as long as others, but he was a blessed man. He was a man who had overwhelming victory even in the midst of sickness. He never allowed fear to overpower him. He walked by faith, never complained, and was always a pleasure to be around. This young man's courageous character will abide in your hearts forever.

Mighty men of great character have journeyed God's earth for less than forty years and have left indelible marks forever in the hearts of many. All these men were God's sons who fulfilled God's purposes. John the Baptist was God's son who committed himself solely to the advancement of God's kingdom. Martin Luther King Jr. was God's son whose words touched the conscience of this nation and the world. God's only begotten Son, Jesus, suffered and died that you and I could be redeemed.

When we look at the short life of Jesus, we can see the strategic work of the Father. God strategically placed Jesus with a mother who served Him no matter the consequences. God strategically placed brothers in Jesus's life that would write the books of James and Jude. As intimately involved as God was in His only begotten Son's life, so was God intimately involved in Devonte's life.

God gave Devonte a mother who placed all her trust in the Lord—a praying mother. Even after her soul was pierced, she faithfully looked to the Lord. Devonte's mother surrendered all to God. God gave Devonte a father with unshakable faith—a father that would not abandon him. The Lord blessed him with a brother who stayed by his side—one who spent many days with him. A brother who looked up to him and called him "my big brother." God graced Devonte with a caring wife who did not forsake him in his sickness—a wife who loved him to the core.

SECTION IV: The eulogy concluded with a final word of comfort and a reminder that this young man is in the presence of God.

> *We may not be able to understand why Devonte had to suffer, but the Bible tells me that those who suffer with Christ shall also reign with Him. Devonte suffered with Christ, and now he has entered into the beautiful kingdom of heaven. He will never experience pain again. He will never cry again, for God has wiped away every tear. On April 12, the spirit of Devonte Smith was ushered into the hands of the true and living God. Devonte, God's son, is home, spending eternity with his Big Brother, Jesus Christ.*

EULOGY 4: EVANGELISTIC EULOGY

Alphonso Fraiser

Synopsis: Alfonso was a young man in his forties who fell asleep while driving. There was a huge crowd at his funeral service, and prior to me beginning the eulogy, family and friends reflected on his life. He was a man who had a big heart—a man who touched many lives. Alphonso was an entrepreneur and a loving father. The sanctuary was filled with many who were unsaved, and so the Lord led me to do an evangelistic eulogy. Some may wonder how an evangelistic eulogy ministers to the hearts of the bereaved, but we should always remember that in addition to bringing comfort, God is concerned about the souls of His people. Even in our eulogies, God is seeking souls.

Scripture: John 3:16 (NKJV)
"God so loved the world that He gave His only begotten Son, that whoever believes in Him should not perish but have everlasting life."

Title:
"Destination"

Section I: I began this eulogy with an emphasis on life after death. It was important to explain to the listeners that we all have an eternal destination. It is important to note that this eulogy may seem more like a sermon because very little was said about the deceased in it. However, as mentioned above, his family and loved ones spoke extensively about him during the time of reflection.

> *Have you ever known anyone to take a trip without knowing his or her destination? When we travel, we want to know where we are going and what time we will arrive. Time is very important to most of us, and we sure wouldn't want to waste our time going to a place we have no desire to go.*
>
> *When we arrive at the airport, train station, or bus depot, we need to have a ticket in our hand. The ticket will state the time of departure as well as our destination. Since it is very important to us that we have the right ticket with the correct destination for our short-term trips here on earth, it is also important that we have the right ticket for our eternal destination.*
>
> *Many of us don't realize the importance of our long-term destination. We have placed so much importance on the here and now. We have spent our time focusing on earthly things: acquiring wealth and material things and indulging in the pleasures of this world. We are concerned with the comforts of our earthly abode without regard for life after our earthly existence.*

Section II: I emphasized Jesus being the Way, but I also addressed some of the questions and doubts of unbelievers.

It is not God's desire for us to perish before we have fully prepared for our final destination. Second Peter 3:9 says, "The Lord is not slack concerning his promise, as some count slackness, but is longsuffering toward us, not willing that any should perish but that all should come to repentance" (NKJV). It is the Lord's desire that none shall perish. So how can we know for sure that we will arrive at the correct eternal destination? Well, Jesus said in John 14:6 (NKJV), "I am the way, the truth, and the life. No one comes to the Father except through Me." Jesus is the way into your eternal destination.

Now some of you might be thinking, "I don't want anything to do with a God I cannot see and cannot touch. But, beloved, God is more than sight and touch. God is the breath that you take. God is in your ability to walk and talk. God's presence is all around you. Just open your eyes and see. Others might be thinking, "How can I believe in God when so many bad things happen?" Beloved, look around and see the good. Good things are happening in us and around us daily. There is good in the beauty of a blue sky, good in the miraculous birth of a baby, good in a cool breeze on a hot summer day, beauty in nature—there is good all around. Oh taste and see that the Lord is good.

Section III: Here I began focusing on the main Scripture. I also wanted to emphasize the importance of unbelievers choosing their final eternal destination.

> *"For God so loved the world that He gave His only begotten Son, that whoever believes in Him should not perish but have everlasting life" (John 3:16 NKJV). Jesus is your Way to your eternal destination. But here's the thing, if you are doubtful that Jesus is your ticket to eternity, then I would suggest that you ask Him to reveal Himself to you. I can tell you that He will not deny you such a request. How do I know? Well, I can remember years ago, driving my car on the Northern State Parkway and saying to God, "If you are God, reveal yourself to me." Within three days, I was at a revival service, and it was there that I gave my soul and life to God. God showed up mightily that day and ever since.*
>
> *God had a plan for my life, and when I sought Him, God revealed His plans to me. God has a plan for your life, but many of us are not walking in God's divine plan because we want to maintain control and charter our own course. But God is a merciful God. It does not matter the path you have taken in life, if you call on the name of the Lord, He will answer you and redirect your path.*
>
> *Jesus is that invaluable ticket to eternal life, and there is nothing—no one—more valuable. Apart from Jesus, we are*

separated from the Father. The Bible asks what good it is to gain the world and lose your soul (see Mark 8:36).

In the book My Descent Into Death by Howard Storm, the author recalls his experience as an atheist who suddenly became ill and died. He recalls how he could see himself outside of his body, and he could see his wife sitting in the hospital chair with her head hung low. He kept calling her, but she could not hear him. It's a long story, but he then found himself in what would be his final destination: a place where he faced great torment and pain.

Eventually he saw a glimpse of a speck of light, and he heard from deep within himself the command to pray. This man could barely remember a prayer. He had spent his life not believing in God, but as the darkness became greater, he began to pray a prayer he remembered praying at seven years old. He said every prayer he could think of including Psalm 23. He even recited "The Star Spangled Banner." He recognized the more he called on God, the more the tormentors decreased until he finally cried out, "Jesus, help me!" That glimpse of light became greater and greater, and he was enveloped in the arms of Jesus Christ. He said that he had never experienced such love in his life. The Lord brought him into His immense love. That atheist was revived from death by the power of God and is alive today to proclaim the truth about Jesus Christ—His grace, mercy, and immeasurable love for us all.

Section IV: Here I provided a final exhortation and a call to surrender their lives to God.

In this celebration of life service, God is still calling your name. He wants you to experience the richness of His love, peace, and joy. God has given you life on this earth, but He also wants to give you life face-to-face with Him. Don't miss out on the greatest blessing God has ever presented to humanity—God's Son, Jesus Christ. Don't miss out on your destination with Him eternally.

Our time here on earth is short compared to our time in eternity. The Lord is calling you into God's eternal love today. It does not matter the path you have taken in life. The Bible tells us that while Jesus was dying on the cross, in between two thieves, one cursed Him and died and the other asked Him to remember him when He came into His kingdom. Jesus answered, "Today you will be with Me in Paradise" (Luke 23:43 NKJV). It didn't matter what kind of life the thief lived; what mattered was he acknowledged God, and God in all His love accepted him into God's eternal kingdom.

Beloved, today God is saying, "All that is required is a repentant heart, one who is willing to say, 'I'm sorry for my sins.'" God is looking for a humble heart. God says, "I love you with an everlasting love, and even though you may not know me or comprehend my love, I still love you. I long for you to come to me." The wages of our sin is eternal death, but the gift of God is eternal life. You can decide on your destination right here and now. Harden not your heart. You may not know the time of your departure, but you can be sure about your destination.

Today, the Lord says, "Seek me and you will find me. Come to me with your questions. I will not turn away from you, but rather I will come to you. If you just talk to me, I will lead you in a relationship with me." We have all been given a free gift—free entrance into the kingdom of God. We don't have to pay for it. We don't have to barter for it. Entrance is not based on how good you have been or how many good things you have done: We can't be good enough to get this ticket on our own. To enter into your eternal divine destination with God, all you have to do is believe in your heart and confess with your mouth that Jesus is Lord. Today, God says, "I have given you heaven's Golden Ticket—free of charge. I have given you my only begotten Son." Jesus has already paid the price; your sins are already forgiven, and your path to God has been made clear. Today God says, "Here He is—accept Jesus into your life, and you will be with me in Paradise." Which ticket are you holding? What's your final destination?

EULOGY 5

Gregory Garrison

Synopsis: Gregory was 64 years of age when he passed away.

Scripture: Psalm 55:22 (NIV)
"Cast your cares on the Lord and he will sustain you."

Title:
"The Heart of a Father"

Section I: I began this eulogy speaking about the deceased. He was a loving father, and I thought it was important to begin the eulogy highlighting his wonderful, fatherly character. This would eventually segue into how our heavenly Father is the most loving father.

> *Brother Gregory "Greg" Garrison was a tenderhearted man with a quiet demeanor. He enjoyed cooking, and he loved to barbecue. You all may remember his delicious homemade turkey burgers, steaks, and hot dogs. He was a master chef who cooked the best baked beans, corn on the cob, macaroni and cheese, and don't forget his special fruit punch. Brother Garrison enjoyed bringing happiness to all through food.*
>
> *But not only did he express his love with food, he also*

always made sure that he was there for his children. Spending quality time with his children was very important to him. He was not only a provider, but he was a hands-on, involved dad. He was the kind of father who would wake up early in the morning just to take his son Timothy fishing. They would spend the entire day together talking and bonding. When Timothy played in his basketball leagues, Gregory would be there cheering him on.

Gregory was a great father to his son, but he was also a wonderful father to his daughter. Gregory was the kind of father that would create sketches for his daughter Mia's school projects. He was the kind of dad that would sell the most candy for her school fundraisers. Gregory was a present father, one who would always be there, proudly cheering his daughter on during her dance recitals. He was that kind of a father.

Section II: It is here that I make the correlation between Gregory's fatherly attributes and our heavenly Father's character.

Gregory was a good man and a wonderful father. He would always say to his children, "Take care of yourself." He only wanted the best for them. His heart was filled with love for them. Your heavenly Father's heart is filled with love for you. The Father's heart is open to you. As you pour out your pain and sorrows in God's presence, God will embrace you with His love. Our heavenly Father cares and loves each of us unconditionally.

In times like this, when the pain is so intense and there is anguish deep within your soul, your heavenly Father will step into that place of darkness, isolation, and grief. God will hold you and comfort you. God will take care of you.

Section III: In this section, I began to expound on the focused Scripture. For further clarity and emphasis, it is always a good practice to provide definitions of key words in the text.

The psalmist said in Psalm 55:22 (NIV), "Cast your cares on the Lord and he will sustain you." This is God's encouragement to you all today. As we draw closer to the Lord, God lifts the burden of grief from our shoulders. God will actually carry our burdens for us. Psalm 68:19 (NIV) says, "Praise be to the Lord, to God our Savior, who daily bears our burdens."

God wants us to cast our cares upon Him. The Hebrew word for cast in this Scripture means "to

throw out, down or away" or "to hurl."[12] It means that

---

12 Strong's Concordance, "7993. Shalak," accessed November, 2024, on BibleHub

God wants us to release every pain and concern. Throw off the burden of grief—throw it to God. God will carry it. That means that we can pour out our deepest feelings and pains to the Lord. God can handle your sorrow, anger, despair, and disappointments. God is strong and mighty. God is your very present help in a time of trouble. Our Father is so awesome—there is not a tear that drops from our eyes that God does not bottle in heaven. Psalm 56:8 (NLT) says, "You keep track of all my sorrows. You have collected all my tears in your bottle. You have recorded each one in your book." Our heavenly Father sees and takes note of all our sorrows. God is concerned.

Section IV: I concluded with a focus on my main point, which was reminding attendees that the heart of our heavenly Father is filled with love.

Gregory's heart was filled with love for his children, and our heavenly Father's heart is filled with love for us. God will be there for you in the midnight hours to hold you, wipe your tears, calm your fears, and commune with you. God will not turn His back on you. God's love is greater than you can ever imagine. The heart of your heavenly Father is filled with compassion, and as you walk through this valley of sorrow, God will be right there leading you to a place of peace and assurance.

---

https://biblehub.com/hebrew/7993.htm

HEALER OF A BROKEN HEART

Your good Father will lead you to a place where you can declare, "Surely His goodness and mercy has followed me all the days of my life." Cast your cares on the Lord, and He will sustain you. God will uphold you. God will help you during the most difficult times. God will not allow your sorrows to overtake you. Your heavenly Father's heart is open to you. Your heavenly Father says, "Come in and let me wrap you with my love." Your heavenly Father is watching over you.

Chapter 6

ELDERLY

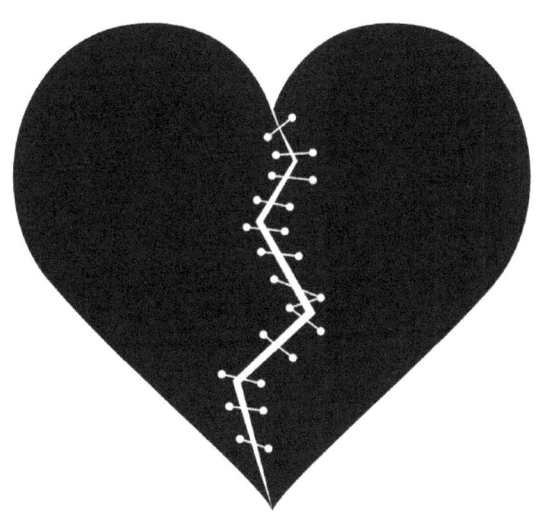

ELDERLY

When the matriarchs and patriarchs of our families pass away, grief is inevitable. It does not matter that they may have lived a full life; loved ones will always grieve the loss of the elderly. I remember ministering to a woman who lost her mother at the age of one hundred three. This woman was in such deep grief, and I said to her, "You have had her in your life for so many years. You have so many memories to grieve." As I said these words to her, I could tell that there was a sense of relief because someone understood her grief. As ministers we must empathize with all. We must be mindful not to dismiss a person's grief or encourage them to "get over it." We are called to journey with them in their grief.

EULOGY 1

Isabella Williams

Synopsis: Isabella passed away suddenly. Sudden deaths can be jarring no matter the age of the deceased.

Scripture: Ecclesiastes 3:1 (NIV)
"There is a time for everything, and a season for every activity under the heavens."

Title:
"God's Time"

Section I: I began this eulogy with words of comfort. Words of comfort are akin to stroking someone's back during a difficult time. The sorrow does not go away, but they somehow feel a little better.

> *There is so much we don't understand about God. Yet we are called to trust God in the most unexpected circumstances. If we were to be honest, we would say that God's timing seems to be off. When we think about the passing of Sister Isabella, God's timing seems off. She was living a good life, and her family was her delight and joy. At age seventy-one, Sister Isabella had the courage to find love again and jump the broom. She was enjoying her new life and journey with her husband.*

In situations like this, God's timing seems off.

Now, while it seems as if this was the most inopportune time for the Lord to receive Isabella in heaven, God—in His sovereignty—has called His daughter home. She went home to a beautiful place of peace, joy, and rest. Even though you are going to miss her presence, find comfort in knowing that she is present with the Lord. She is present with God, the One that we cannot see with our natural eyes; yet Isabella can now behold God face-to-face. Her passing may seem untimely, but God is sovereign—God is in control of all things and orchestrates time.

Section II: It is here that the main Scripture was brought to light. I wanted to be intentional about focusing on my main point, which was that God's timing does not always equate to our timing.

God's time is the focus of our text. Most scholars say that the book of Ecclesiastes was written by King Solomon, who was believed to be one the wisest kings. In this book of wisdom, King Solomon pens words that cause the reader to pause and reflect. It is in this text that he tells us that there is a time for everything under God's purpose. The Scripture tells us that under heaven there is "a time to be born and a time to die" (3:2 NIV). It tells us that there is "a time to weep, and a time to laugh; a time to mourn and a time to dance" (3:4 NIV). Under heaven there is "a time to embrace and a time to refrain from embracing" (3:5 NIV). In life there is a time for everything, and while God's timing is difficult for us to understand, we can find comfort in knowing that during the storms of life, we can hold on to God's unchanging hand and to God's promises.

Jesus's promise to us in John 14:1–3 (NKJV) is "let not your heart be troubled [disturbed, terrified, thrown into confusion] . . . I go to prepare a place for you . . . that where I am, there you may be also." Jesus spoke these words to His disciples because He knew that His time on earth was almost up. He spoke these words because He knew that after His death, resurrection, and ascension, the disciples would experience difficult times. Jesus was on the cusp of accomplishing all the Father planned for Him to do, and while it all seemed untimely for the disciples, this moment was God's perfect timing.

Section III: I concluded with words of comfort for the bereaved. They needed to be reminded that God's timing was perfect for Isabella's homegoing. Staying true to the Ecclesiastes text, I spoke words of comfort reminding them that in time God will make all things beautiful—even their grief.

It was Isabella's time to go home. She had accomplished

all that her Father willed for her to do. She labored in God's vineyard for many years, and now Jesus has prepared a room for her. It was her time to enter into God's glorious presence.

In God's time, what was once bitter will become sweet. In God's time, our mourning will turn to joy. In God's time, broken hearts will be mended. In God's time, our wounds will be healed. In God's time, tears will turn to laughter. In God's time, God will shine His light into our darkness. You may not be able to see it now or understand how God is going to do it, but God will make everything beautiful in its time.

EULOGY 2

Ethel Swanson

Synopsis: Ethel spent years bedridden before she passed away.

Scripture: Psalm 55:6 (NIV)
"And I said, 'Oh, that I had the wings of a dove! I would fly away and be at rest.'"

Title:
"I Have an Interest Over There"

Section I: I began this eulogy with an illustration about a bird with clipped wings and connected it to the difficulties that some people face in life. There are people who spend several years incapacitated because of an infirmity. Ethel Swanson was one of those people—she was bedridden for more than twenty years.

> *Recently I visited a nursing home. They had a bird that would come out and sit on the top of its cage. When the little bird got tired of sitting, she would go back inside the cage. I asked one of the workers, "Can the bird fly around?" She replied, "No, we clipped her wings so that she can't fly around."*

ELDERLY

In this journey called life, it seems that some people have to live with clipped wings due to an illness. There are some who can no longer move around and do the things they would like to do. Some are incapacitated, but the good news is that there will come a day when the suffering is all over and the person in Christ is set free into eternity with the Lord.

Section II: This section made the connection between the bird with clipped wings and Sister Swanson's condition before her passing.

Bedridden for more than twenty years, Ethel Swanson was like the clipped wing bird. After a while, she grew very weary and wanted God to take her home. She would always say, "I have an interest over there."

Her comment reminded me of the song "Precious Lord, Take My Hand"—a song that speaks of a tired, sorrowful soul in need of God's relief. Sister Swanson was weary and wanted to go home, and God took her hand.

Today, she has been released from her ailing body, and she has been made whole. The Word of God tells us that "Many are the afflictions of the righteous, But the Lord delivers him out of them all" (Psalm 34:19 NKJV). God has set her free from her bed of affliction.

Section III: This section began to focus on Sister Swanson's faith even in the midst of affliction.

What I loved about Sister Swanson was that she never lost her hope in her God. She worshiped God even though, like the bird with the clipped wings, her quality of life was not what she wanted it to be. She worshiped the Lord in her long-suffering. She worshiped the Lord in spite of her affliction. Why? Because in the midst of her weariness, Sister Swanson had a vision.

She believed that her situation would not last forever and that one day God was going to bring about a great deliverance in her life. She believed that her present suffering would not compare to the glory she was going to receive. She could envision herself walking again. She could actually see her deliverance. Sister Swanson remained focused on her inheritance. She knew that she was going to a place where there would be no more pain and suffering. She could see "over there"—the place where her heavenly Father would wipe away all her tears. She remained focused on God's promise that there was a mansion awaiting her, prepared by her Lord and Savior, Jesus Christ.

Today, she leaves a legacy. She leaves a legacy of unwavering trust in God. She leaves a legacy that reminds us to remain faithful to God, no matter what comes our way. Sister Swanson taught us how to wait on the Lord. She taught us that even when you cannot physically stand, you can stand in your faith and stand on what you believe. She taught us to remain steadfast, unmovable, always abounding in the work of the Lord, for our labor is not in vain. She taught us the greatest lesson of all—remain faithful, for you shall reap if you faint not.

Section IV: At this point, I briefly expounded on the biblical text. I also connected David's yearning to fly away to Sister Swanson's yearning to go home to the Lord.

The psalmist King David had his share of affliction, so much so that he wanted to fly away. He exclaimed, "Oh, that I had the wings of a dove! I would fly away and be at rest." (Psalm 55:6 NIV) David wanted to get away from all his troubles, get away from his persistent enemies, get away from the trials of life, and escape his misery. David wanted to escape it all and find rest for his soul.

God gave Sister Swanson wings—wings that would bring her into the fullness of life with Jesus. Like a dove, she has flown away and left every sorrow behind. She has flown off into paradise: no more pain, no more sickness. She is free—unrestricted, unbounded, and living a glorious new life with God.

Section V: I concluded this eulogy with emphasis on Sister Swanson's interest over there. Now, while I did not include a final hymn, oftentimes in closing my eulogies, I would close by reciting a hymn that ties into the focus of the eulogy. For instance, for this particular eulogy, I would recite "I Fly Away." If there is a musician, choir, and/or soloist, they would assist by providing the ministry of music to conclude the eulogy.

> *Jesus said "Come to Me, all you who labor and are heavy laden, and I will give you rest" (Matthew 11:28 NKJV). Sister Swanson has now found true and complete rest for her soul. She is at rest from all her labors and toils. Sister Swanson is now in the presence of Jesus Christ, her Lord.*
>
> *She had an "interest over there." She knew that in glory she would be reunited with her mother and other loved ones. Over there is where she knew she would see Jesus. Over there, Sister Swanson walks on the streets of gold. "And I said, 'Oh, that I had the wings of a dove! I would fly away and be at rest" (Psalm 55:6 NIV). Like a dove, she has flown over there—over there, where she finds eternal rest.*

EULOGY 3

Lillian Card

Synopsis: Sister Lillian passed away after battling a long-term illness.

Scripture: Romans 8:16–18 (NIV)
"The Spirit himself testifies with our spirit that we are God's children. Now if we are children, then we are heirs—heirs of God and co-heirs with Christ, if indeed we share in his sufferings in order that we may also share in his glory."

"I consider that our present sufferings are not worth comparing with the glory that will be revealed in us."

Title:
"She Made It to the Throne Room"

Section I: I had the pleasure of visiting Sister Lillian for several years. She was such a trouper in spite of the many setbacks with her health. Following her passing, I sat with her family to discover more about their beloved Sister Lillian. I began this eulogy with a focus on her life.

> *Sister Lillian Card loved to be outdoors. In her later days, she took pleasure in a simple walk around the block— that time was precious to her. She loved her neighborhood,*

and she loved the children in the neighborhood. They were always welcome into her home, welcome to eat from her refrigerator and always welcome to her delicious ice tea. Sister Lillian loved spending time with the children, but she also loved to cook.

Everything she made was delicious. Family and friends loved her collard greens, fried chicken, sweet potato pies, potato salad, and her famous biscuits with the butter and syrup on top. She could cook it all and cooked it well, but what she was most known for was her Jesus Cake—a recipe she got from her daughter Deborah. She called it the Jesus Cake because with every bite, all you could say was "Jesus." That's how good it was.

Yes, Sister Lillian was a great cook, but she not only loved to cook, she was also adventurous. She loved to travel on cruises and even swam with sharks. She was a brave woman. In fact, her son, Allan, would fondly say to her, "You are a tough ol' bird."

She was definitely a tough cookie. I don't know how many trips she took to the hospital, but she handled it with a grain of salt, and she never complained. She and I would talk about her suffering experiences, pray about her troubles, and sing to the Lord, and eventually any sorrow would turn to joy. That was Sister Lillian: She transformed in the presence of the Lord.

ELDERLY

Sister Lillian was an awesome woman. A stay-at-home mom for ten years, she walked her daughter Renee back and forth to school every day. While she wasn't an overly affectionate woman, she knew how to express her love, and Renee would say that she was the best mother ever.

With beautiful brown eyes and a smile that we will never forget, Sister Lillian knew just how to keep you laughing. I would always laugh when she referred to Sloan Kettering Hospital (a hospital for cancer patients) as her "getaway hotel." She was a woman who could find humor in the midst of suffering. In the midst of sickness, she kept her faith. She loved the Lord with all her being, and she trusted God through it all. She depended on God for she knew within her soul that she was not forsaken by her heavenly Father.

She was a woman of faith, and even in her last days on this earth, Sister Lillian interceded for others. She asked God to touch and heal others. In those moments, I believe the Lord looked upon her and said, "This is my daughter with whom I'm pleased, whom I love."

The Word of God was embedded in her soul, and in spite of the pain, in spite of the suffering, in spite of the separation from her loved ones, she worshiped God. She was a worshiper who would love to sing to the Lord. She loved the hymns and gospel music, and would listen to songs like "Nobody Greater," "Amazing Grace," and "Take Me to the King" over and over again.

In the midst of her suffering and pain, Sister Lillian would cry out to the "King of Glory!" Although she didn't want to be separated from her loved ones, she knew her time had come, and she wanted to be with the King. For us today, we are in the midst of our own pain, grief, and sorrow, but we can follow Sister Lillian's example and cry out, "Take me to the King." It is in the presence of the King that we can receive solace and relief.

Section II: Here I transitioned into the focused text and connected the Word of God to Sister Lillian's suffering and present glory.

The people that the apostle Paul wrote to in Romans 8:16–18 were experiencing great suffering. Paul writes, "The Spirit himself testifies with our spirit that we are God's children. Now if we are children, then we are heirs—heirs of God and co-heirs with Christ, if indeed we share in his sufferings in order that we may also share in his glory."

"I consider that our present sufferings are not worth comparing with the glory that will be revealed in us" (NIV).

Paul knew what it felt like to suffer. While serving God,

he was frequently imprisoned, severely flogged, beaten with rods, pelted with stones, shipwrecked, and exposed to death innumerable times. Paul was acquainted with tremendous suffering, but he recognized that the pain that he and the suffering saints experienced could not compare to the glory that would be revealed in them in the coming age.

He told the saints then and he is telling us now that we are children of the Most High God and joint heirs with Christ. What's our inheritance? God's most wonderful glory. Merriam-Webster defines the word glory as "a state of great gratification or exaltation, a height of prosperity or achievement, great beauty and splendor (magnificence)."[13]

Sister Lillian has been taken into glory. Her weeping may have endured for a night, but joy—unspeakable joy—has come her way. She has been glorified with Christ. On December 27, she died in this world of pain and suffering and was reborn into a world of eternal health, strength, and beauty. She walked by faith here, but in paradise, she walks by sight in God's glory.

---

13 Merriam-Webster Dictionary, "glory," accessed September 25, 2024, https://www.merriam-webster.com/dictionary/glory.

Section III: I concluded by reiterating the eulogy's title and focusing on the fact that Sister Lillian made it to the throne room.

> *Lillian Card is in the throne room of God. Can you imagine what it's like for her in the presence of the Lord? The brilliance of God's glory has engulfed her very soul. She is no longer burned out from the cares of this world: no more feeble legs, no need for a cane or a walker. She is free from every care, every worry—no more stress and no more pain.*
>
> *She is in the throne room. She no longer has to sing "Take Me to the King." She is with the King. She is in the King of Kings' throne room. She is in the place that Jesus calls paradise. She is in the perpetual presence of the King of Glory. The throne room is where she will have lasting joy. Sister Lillian made it into the throne room! Hallelujah!*

EULOGY 4

Oscar Johnson

Synopsis: Oscar Johnson, who was 92 years old, did not have a relationship with his daughter prior to his death. This presented a unique situation for me, since his daughter knew almost nothing about him and could not provide substantial information. The only thing she knew was his occupation and one of his hobbies. Yet she was doing her best to give him an honorable service. It was then my task to write a eulogy that honored Mr. Johnson and glorified God. As I surrendered it all, I was intrigued that the Holy Spirit directed me to preach "Honor Thy Father."

Scripture: Ephesians 6:2–3 (NIV)
"'Honor your father and mother'—which is the first commandment with a promise—'so that it may go well with you and that you may enjoy long life on the earth.'"

Title:
"Honor Your Father"

Section I: I began with a relatable story taken from the book of Genesis about forgiveness and honoring one's parents.

> *For every individual who has been brought into a personal relationship with God, the command is simple*

and clear: We are to honor God, and just as we are to honor the heavenly Father, so are we to honor those who were divinely chosen to birth us into the earth—our fathers and mothers.

There is a story in Genesis (25:9) that is a great example of a child honoring a parent. The story is about Ishmael's choice to honor his father, Abraham, after his death. You see, the Bible does not tell us that Ishmael and his father had a relationship. In fact, Ishmael was sent away by his father to live in the wilderness with his single mother, Hagar. Ishmael was the outcast, while his brother Isaac was the chosen one who lived with his father. As far as Ishmael was concerned, Abraham was an absentee dad. He wasn't there to see him grow to become a man. He wasn't there to help him during difficult times. Abraham was not present in his son's life. But, in spite of it all, the Bible tells us that Ishmael was there for the commemoration and burial of his father. Ishmael honored his father, Abraham.

Now, while we don't know why Ishmael chose to honor Abraham, perhaps he was told at some point about God's promised blessings in Genesis 17:20 (NIV), "And as for Ishmael, I have heard you: I will surely bless him; I will make him fruitful and will greatly increase his numbers. He will be the father of twelve rulers, and I will make him into a great nation." Perhaps it was just his good nature. We do not know his reasons for honoring his father, but what we do know is that Ishmael could have chosen to be bitter, resentful, and unforgiving. But instead, he chose to love his father.

SECTION II: At this point, the biblical text is brought into focus.

Ephesians 6:2–3 (NIV) says, " 'Honor your father and mother'—which is the first commandment with a promise—'so that it may go well with you and that you may enjoy a long life on the earth.' " This commandment comes with an irrevocable promise: When we honor our parents, God's blessings of a long, abundant life will be our portion. God not only wants us to have eternal life, but God wants us to have life and life more abundantly here on earth.

God's promise is that when we honor our mothers and fathers, it will be well with us. We will live well, be fruitful, and have joy. The promise is that we will live long, prosperous lives here on earth. I think that's good news because the reality is that some people live long, miserable, painful, bitter lives. There are some who say, "I will never forgive my father and/or mother for what they did." There are some who die angry with an unforgiving heart.

SECTION III: At this point, I wanted to highlight the importance of forgiveness. I also included a part of my own personal journey toward honoring my father. I felt that it was very important to be transparent in this eulogy. Transparency created a shared connection with the listeners. In essence, I wanted them to know that I was not simply preaching it, but I lived it.

> *But forgiveness is a powerful thing. It has the power to free us from the chains of resentment, anger, and hostility. Forgiveness sets us free to live the way God intends for us to live, to live a life filled with joy, peace, and love. Forgiveness is powerful, but it can be difficult, and when it is, we can call upon the Almighty God to step into our hearts to give us the strength to let it all go.*
>
> *It was God who had to step into my heart when I could not forgive my father. My father was an absentee dad, and when the Lord instructed me to call him, my response was "Why should I call my father? He has never been a father to me!" I remember it so clearly, one day the Lord replied, "And you have never been a daughter to him." That was the day that I called my father, and so began a new daughter-father relationship. And here's the thing that I will never forget: On that day, my father prayed the prayer of salvation with me.*
>
> *Even if our mothers and fathers are no longer living, we can, and should, honor them. We do this by speaking*

well of them to others. Whatever they did or did not do, we must make the decision to let it go. Ephesians 6:2–3 reminds us that things will go well with us when we honor our parents and let go of past hurts. This means that we could see generational cycles of absentee fathers and mothers broken in our families. Honoring our parents frees our hearts to live and trust others deeply. This act of obedience to God is an example to loved ones who will follow suit. In fact, that's what happened to me. When I forgave my father, my siblings followed suit. When we let it all go and honor our parents, we can lie down in sweet rest and peace. There is an abundance of blessings in honoring those who were chosen to birth us into this world.

SECTION IV: I closed this eulogy with a pronunciation of blessing upon all in attendance.

Oscar Johnson may not have been there throughout the years for his family, especially his daughter, but today you all honor him. So, today I pray this blessing upon your lives: May the blessings of the Lord overtake you. May the Lord bless you and keep you. May the Lord make his face shine on you and be gracious to you. May the Lord turn His face toward you and give you peace. Amen.

EULOGY 5

Beatrice Mae Evans

Synopsis: While I cannot remember the details surrounding her passing, she was an older woman who lived a fruitful life.

Scripture: 2 Timothy 4:7-8 (NIV)
"I have fought the good fight, I have finished the race, I have kept the faith. Now there is in store for me the crown of righteousness, which the Lord, the righteous Judge, will award to me on that day—and not only to me, but also to all who have longed for his appearing."

Title:
"The Baton of Prayer"

SECTION I: I began this eulogy with a focus on the life of the deceased—a life that spanned two centuries.

> *On November 13, 1911, Beatrice Mae Evans entered into the twentieth century and lived on into the twenty-first century. She witnessed the roaring twenties, World Wars I and II, the Korean conflict, Desert Storm, the years of the big bands, the Depression, the fall of the stock market, the emergence of Social Security, the Civil Rights movement, affirmative action, segregation, integration, and the World Trade Center tragedy. And most importantly, she lived to see a black man, Barack*

ELDERLY

Obama, run for and win the United States presidential election. Beatrice had seen it all. Her life was a living testimony of the Lord's goodness.

As a little child, Sister Beatrice played the drums in her Pentecostal church home. She was always willing to lend a helping hand; as she got older, she worked in the soup kitchen serving the needy. Her childhood was not easy—Beatrice faced many obstacles—but even then, her faith in God helped her to overcome every trial. When we think about it, Sister Beatrice could have been bitter about some of the things that were done to her, but she became a better person because of it. She loved God, and she demonstrated her love for Him in her everyday life.

She was a woman of faith who knew how to seek God with all her heart and soul. She was a forgiving woman with a wonderful heart. She did everything for her family. She nursed her mother, sister, brother, and daughter during their times of affliction. She was the family's seamstress, sewing Easter outfits and casual clothing for all. She even taught her grandchildren how to sew, knit, and crochet. She was Nana, who helped raise her grandchildren and great-grandchildren. Sister Beatrice loved all her family, and she fought for them daily in prayer.

A mighty bondage breaker, God had anointed Sister

Beatrice to be a powerful warrior in prayer. She not only fought for her family, but she fought for friends and strangers on her knees. With her weapon of prayer, she witnessed the deliverance of family members from substance abuse and dysfunctional behaviors. She lived to see the fruit of her labor, as many were not only delivered but were saved through faith in Jesus.

Sister Beatrice kept her family together. She ran a good race, and now she has finished her course. She may no longer be with us, but she has left an indelible mark on this earth. She may not go down in the history books like Harriet Tubman, Jarena Lee, or Sojourner Truth, but her name is written in your hearts. She ran well and has now passed through her earthly finish line. She has been given her heavenly reward.

SECTION II: It is at this point I transitioned from speaking about the deceased to focusing on the main biblical text.

There is a crown awaiting the saints of God. Second Timothy 4:7–8 (NIV) says, "I have fought the good fight, I have finished the race, I have kept the faith. Now there is in store for me the crown of righteousness, which the Lord, the righteous Judge, will award to me on that day—and not only to me, but also to all who have longed for his appearing." Paul ran the race of faith. He endured the pain and kept the faith because he knew that he would receive a crown that was different from the customary crowns of his time. In that era, wreaths made of olive branches were given as prizes in military and athletic competitions. Paul was not looking forward to a man-made prize. He looked forward to receiving an imperishable prize: the crown of righteousness.

SECTION III: The concluding sections connected Sister Beatrice's life of prayer to Paul's persistence in the race of faith. I concluded with an encouragement for the attendees to grab a hold of the baton of prayer passed on by Sister Beatrice.

Like Paul, Sister Beatrice ran a good race. She ran the race of faith, and now she has passed on the baton of prayer. It is this baton of prayer that will carry you through the joys and trials of life. Look at the path she has made for you, her loved ones. She has shown you how to live with God and for God. She has taught you how to trust God in spite of the circumstances. Grab hold of the baton of prayer and keep your eyes on the finish line. Keep the faith in the midst of darkness, and God will show you the light at the end of the tunnel.

Grab hold of the baton of prayer and run your course. As Sister Beatrice persevered through prayer, you too must stay faithful and persevere. You will reap if you don't faint. Even when life gets rough, pray. Hold on to the baton and keep running. Pray when you are weary.

Pray when you are sad. Pray for loved ones. Pray for opportunities to serve others with your time and talent. The reward is an awesome one. Your inheritance is beyond what you could ever imagine. Run your race well and hold on to the baton of prayer. Hold on to the legacy of Beatrice Mae Evans. Fight on your knees. Fight for your family. Pray for future generations. Pray and don't stop praying.

THE CONCLUSION

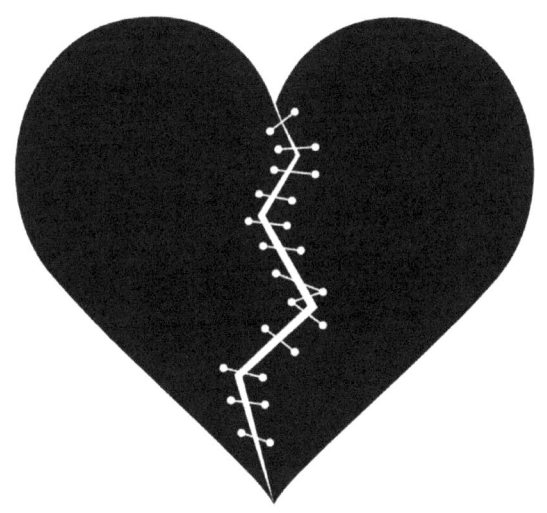

FINAL EULOGY

I conclude this book with one of my favorite eulogies. I have revised and preached this eulogy countless times. It is one that is near and dear to my heart. I close with this not only because it is the title of the book but because it's the crux of this book: God is and continues to be the healer of broken hearts.

As ministers, now more than ever, we are called to be beacons of hope. I have personally witnessed how this eulogy has brought hope to many. Now it's your time. God has anointed you to be a healer of broken hearts. Know that each time you are assigned to preach a eulogy for grieving souls, you are doing your part to mend their hearts. So pray, hear, write, and preach. Here is "Healer of a Broken Heart."

Healer of a Broken Heart

Scripture: Psalm 147:3 (NIV)
"He heals the brokenhearted and binds up their wounds."

When we lose a loved one, our souls are in turmoil. The pain is extremely deep, the heart is crushed, and the mind is overwhelmed. Our souls are downcast in times like these.

We wish that it was only a dream, but we wake up each morning to a reality that our lives have been changed. Our reality is filled with memories and deep emotions of grief.

Lionel will always be a part of your lives, and your love for him will never fade. You will always remember his heart of compassion. You will always remember how he loved to tell jokes and make you all laugh. You will remember the stories he told about his childhood and how he enjoyed being with his family. Lionel loved his family, but he also loved his car. It gave him pleasure to spend hours washing, shining, and perfecting his Ladybug every Saturday morning. You will hold onto the memories of Thanksgiving fried turkey and his Christmas ham. You will remember Lionel, and sometimes those memories will make you feel as if your hearts are being broken all over again, but that's when you need heaven to mend your broken hearts.

Only God can heal the broken pieces of your heart and mend it back together. Only God can give you peace of mind. God's grace

THE CONCLUSION

is sufficient for you. Only God can be your present help in a time of trouble. The children of Israel needed God's help and healing. Psalm 147:3 (NIV) says, "He heals the brokenhearted and binds up their wounds." The Israelites needed God's reassurance in the midst of their brokenness. This text was a promise to an exiled nation that was broken by their captivity. God's promise to God's people was that He would heal their grief and return them to their homeland, Jerusalem. God did not turn away God's people when they needed Him but instead turned to them with a promise of comfort, healing, and restoration. God has not turned away from you in your darkest hour. God sees your pain and your grief, and it is God's promise to heal your broken hearts.

Grief can be overwhelming. Grief will challenge your faith. Grief can lead us into destructive habits. If we are not careful, we will turn to the bottle to soothe our pain. Depression and deep sorrow will attempt to keep us bedbound, sleeping our lives away in an attempt to escape the pain. We need God to heal us. You can't heal your broken heart by yourself, but if you allow God into your darkest space, the Father of lights will shine within and bring hope in the midst of your grief. I like to use the acrostic OWN when I think about our dependence on God for our healing.

- **O**—In our season of grief, we must **open** our hearts up to God. Just as one in the natural world would need heart surgery for healing, so too we must allow God to perform open-heart surgery so that we may be healed from our grief. When we open up to God, we will hear from God and receive the strength and encouragement to face each day. When you open your heart up to God and call on God in your distress, God will not leave you comfortless. Open your heart up to God and the Lord will restore hope. The Lord will give you peace that surpasses all understanding and restore your zeal for the future. Open your heart up to the Healer, and God will guard your heart and mind through Christ Jesus.

- **W—Weep** in the presence of God. When our hearts are shattered, weeping in our heavenly Father's presence is a form of prayer. Psalm 56:8 (NLT) says, "You keep track of all my sorrows. You have collected all my tears in your bottle. You have recorded each one in your book." Think about that. God has collected all your tears in heaven. God is aware and concerned about every painful tear that has flowed down your cheeks. In the midst of your darkest times, God is right there with you. Weep in the presence of God. Psalm 30:5 reminds us that "weeping may endure for a night, But joy comes in the morning" (NKJV). You may be weeping now, but eventually joy will come. God will turn your sorrows into joy and your despair into praise. Weep before the Lord, and God will renew your strength.

- **N**—We **need** God more than ever before in our seasons of grief. In the words of hymnist Annie Sherwood Hawks, "I need Thee, O I need Thee; every hour I need Thee! O bless me, now my Savior, I come to Thee." You cannot heal yourself. This pain is too deep, but when you turn to God, the Lord will do what He promised according to God's Word. God will heal your broken heart. God will give you peace that surpasses all understanding. God is a loving God, full of compassion and mercy. God's faithfulness reaches to the heavens, and God is rich in love. Rely on God's goodness in the midst of your grief. Put all your trust in the Lord. God will sustain you. God will comfort you. God will help you.

You have a heavenly Father who wants to embrace you with His love. God wants to enter into that deep place of pain and pour out His strength and peace upon you. God wants to hold you in His loving arms and embrace you with His heart. God's grace is sufficient for you. God will be your present help in times of trouble. God is your Healer. God will restore your soul. Open your heart to God, weep in His presence, recognize your need for Him, and God will heal your broken heart.

FINAL THOUGHTS

I titled this book *Healer of a Broken Heart* because over the years, I have watched, with joy, the Word manifested in the lives of many. I have witnessed God in miraculous ways. I have witnessed God impart new dreams, new ideas, and a reason to go on in the hearts of those who have lost loved ones. I have witnessed the bereaved shed their cloak of deep grief and take on the cloak of hope. I have witnessed over a period of time weeping turn to joy. I have seen how loved ones come out on the other side of grief stronger and excited about their futures. I have seen expectations restored and hope renewed. I have witnessed lives changed as loved ones draw closer to God and commit their lives to the One who kept their minds and hearts through it all. Truly, God has proven Himself to be the healer of a broken heart.

The bereavement ministry has indeed been a burdensome joy, and God has been faithful through it all. As you go forth, remember that as ministers we are called to preach the Word of God with faith. The eulogy should be something the family can hold on to during their grieving process. It should draw souls into the kingdom of God. The eulogy is that baton of hope for the bereaved, one that they can grab hold of when their soul is overwhelmed with despair. The eulogy is a powerful, life-changing sermon that can make a difference in the lives of the hearers for years to come.

It is my prayer that this book has provided you with the information you need to feel confident in preparing a meaningful, anointed eulogy. Here are some final tips:

- **Family Involvement**: If you are tasked with preparing the funeral program, make sure to get the family involved. This gives loved ones comfort in knowing that they are involved in what will become a precious keepsake.
    - Speak with them about suitable opening hymns or worship songs. Suggest songs that will be sung before the acknowledgments and right before the eulogy. Note that the closing songs are usually upbeat and victorious.
    - Help them choose the appropriate Old and New Testament Scriptures.
    - Help them to select the best picture of the deceased. Make sure that photos are high resolution and are appropriate. In other words, try to encourage loved ones not to provide photos of the deceased wearing revealing clothing, engaging in drinking, or even with sunglasses on their face. We want the best photo that honors the deceased.
- **Suitable Scriptures:** Consider providing a list of Old Testament and New Testament Scriptures. This allows the

family to search through and select appropriate texts.

  - If a family chooses a Scripture or song that is not suitable for a funeral, it is your obligation, as the minister, to explain what the church deems appropriate. For instance, at my church, we only use Christian songs for funeral services. Whatever your church's standards, we must keep the service holy and sacred in the sanctuary. We must always maintain an atmosphere that allows the mighty presence of God to flow in each service.

- **Due Diligence:** There are times when a family may not want to disclose how their loved one died. However, as the minister in charge of the service, we may need to know for safety reasons. For instance, if the deceased was murdered by a gang and/or if the murderer has not been captured, we may need to seek police protection for the family and for ourselves. I may ask the question, "Was your loved one sick for a long time, or was this a sudden death?" If the family isn't willingly providing information, I have even gone so far as to check the news, and from time to time I have found out that the deceased was in fact murdered. Doing your due diligence will help you to plan effectively for a spirit-filled, safe service.

  - It is also good to know if the deceased had a relationship with the Lord. This information will inform the content of the eulogy. For instance, we don't want to preach "To die is gain," if the person never acknowledged Jesus as their Lord and Savior. Note: Our assignment is never to condemn. We are called to be agents of comfort and encouragement.

- **Support After the Funeral:** The bereaved should be supported during and after the service. Consider the following ideas:
    - Bereavement retreats that provide a space for loved ones to share, grieve, and heal together.
    - Annual events like the "Celebrating and Honoring Heavenly Mothers and Children," held the day before Mother's Day and my church's "Blue Christmas" December event will provide comfort and aid in the healing process. Along with food, these events include keynote speakers and great music, creating a space for all to reflect and enjoy.
    - If you haven't yet done so, consider starting a ministry for the grieving members of your church. We currently host a weekly virtual gathering, the Healing Love Bereavement Ministry. This allows church members and our community to receive the support and healing that is needed to move forward in life. In addition, a bereavement ministry presents the opportunity for us to provide comfort to people beyond the physical walls of the church and beyond geographical boundaries.

- **Funeral/Memorial Arrangement Form:** In the appendix of

THE CONCLUSION

this book, I have provided a sample Funeral Arrangement Intake Form. You may download a sample form by using the QR Code on page 164. If you are reading the ebook, click here for your copy.

- o When gathering information, you can email the intake form to the family so that they are aware of what's needed. This further helps them to feel involved in the process.

•••

May the Lord bless you and use you to comfort all who need to be comforted.

"He heals the brokenhearted
and binds up their wounds."
(Psalm 147:3 NIV)

•••

Appendix

RESOURCES

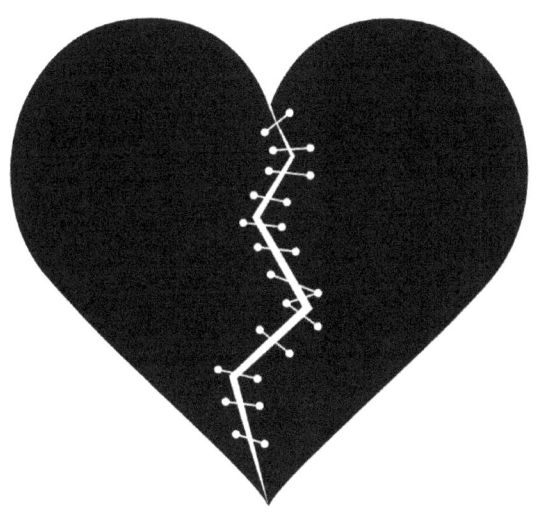

SAMPLE FUNERAL / MEMORIAL ARRANGEMENT FORM

Name of Your Church							
Wake Repast	DATE		YES	NO	**FUNERAL ARRANGEMENTS**		
Funeral Repast	DATE		YES	NO	Funeral Day		
Pastor Notified	DATE		YES	NO	Funeral Date		
Stewardess Notified	DATE		YES	NO	Viewing Time		
Ushers Notified	DATE		YES	NO	Funeral Time		
Security Notified	DATE		YES	NO	Funeral Location		
Communications Notified	DATE		YES	NO			
Name of Deceased:							Age:
Date of Birth:					Date of Death:		
Member:	Yes		No	Resolution:	Yes		No
Ministry 1#			Ministry 2#		Ministry 3#		
If not a member, is there a relative who is a member?				Yes	No		
Nearest Relative:					Relationship:		
Address:							
Contact #:							
Email Address:							
Funeral Home:						Phone #:	
Name of Director:							
Cemetery Location:							
Wake Location:							
Wake Coverage:							
Officiating:				Eulogist:			
Old Testament:				New Testament:			
Obituary Read:	Yes		No	If yes, read by			
Family Tribute:							
Remarks:							
Organist:				Vocalist:			
Opening Song:							
Selection #1:							
Selection #2:							
Recessional Song:							
Video Presentation:		Yes	No				
Still Shot Photo:		Yes	No				
Additional Information:							
Interviewed by:						Date	

NOTES:

- Ministry 1, 2, and 3 refer to clubs and organizations the deceased was a member of.

- Some families may opt for virtual streaming in conjunction with an in-person gathering.
- Still Shot Photo refers to a photo of the deceased that is visible on a screen (if available) during the service.
- As the minister overseeing the funeral or memorial, you may also want to note the name of the printer that will be printing the program, especially if it's outsourced.
- All obituaries should be proofed.

Use the QR Code to download a copy of the memorial form:

THE ORDER OF SERVICE

The Reverend _____, Officiating

The Prelude.. Name of Musician
The Processional
The Final Viewing
The Opening Song ...."Title of Song"
The Prayer of Comfort
The Scripture Reading
   Old Testament –
   New Testament –
The Musical Selection.........."Title of the Song".........Name of Choir or Soloist
The Acknowledgment of Condolences
The Family Tribute...Name of Person(s)
The Resolution
The Obituary..Name of Person
The Musical Selection........."Title of the Song".......Name of Choir or Soloist
The Eulogy..The Reverend_____
The Moments of Meditation
The Closing Prayer
The Benediction
The Recessional Song..."Title of the Song"

The Interment: Name and address of cemetery

NOTES:

- The opening song is typically a congregational hymn or praise song.
- If the deceased is a member of the church, we will include the resolution, which is a resolve of the church written on behalf of the deceased.
- The obituary may be read by a person or read silently while the musician plays softly.

PRAISE BE TO THE GOD
AND FATHER OF OUR LORD
JESUS CHRIST, THE FATHER
OF COMPASSION AND THE
GOD OF ALL COMFORT, WHO
COMFORTS US IN ALL OUR
TROUBLES, SO THAT WE CAN
COMFORT THOSE IN ANY
TROUBLE WITH THE COMFORT
WE OURSELVES RECEIVE
FROM GOD.

2 Corinthians 1:3-4 (NIV)

www.ingramcontent.com/pod-product-compliance
Lightning Source LLC
Chambersburg PA
CBHW052129030426
42337CB00028B/5081